Healing the Heart
Healing the 'Hood

Healing the Heart
Healing the 'Hood

Olgen Williams

Purdue University Press / West Lafayette, Indiana

Library of Congress Cataloging-in-Publication Data
Williams, Olgen, 1948–
Healing the heart, healing the 'hood / Olgen Williams.

p.   cm.

ISBN 1-55753-379-2

1. Williams, Olgen, 1948– 2. African American civic leaders—Indiana—
Indianapolis—Biography. 3. Community development, Urban—United
States—Citizen participation. 4. Community policing—United States—
Case studies. 5. Volunteer workers in community development—United
States--Case studies. 6. Volunteer workers in social service—United
States—Case studies. 7. Inner cities—United States—Case studies.
8. Urban poor—United States—Case studies. 9. Social action—United
States—Case studies. 10. Narcotic addicts—Rehabilitation—
United States. I. Title.

HV40.32.W55A3 2005
307.3'416'092--dc22

2004021995

This book is dedicated

To my Savior Jesus Christ. I would not be the person who I am today if it were not for Him.

To Mary Catherine Williams, my wife and the mother of our eleven children—Angie, Kimberley, Olgen M., Joi, Jason, Timothy, Rebecca, Nicole, Aaron, Jonathan, and David. Mary has been the guide of our home. I love her and our children very much.

To my church, friends, and community, whose faith and trust in me has allowed me to serve them.

Contents

Foreword

Olgen Williams demonstrates that the writing of autobiography can be an act not only of expression but also of healing. He began to write *Healing the Heart* while a student at Indianapolis's Martin University, whose stated mission is to provide a healing and freedom-minded environment.

For over two decades at Martin University, the writing of autobiography was a vital element in the research-based Prior Learning Assessment (PLA) Program, which evaluates and grants credit for out-of-classroom college-level learning. Olgen Williams is among the many students who, with my guidance, completed the PLA process, earned additional credits in the classroom, and received bachelor's degrees.

When I wrote to a number of former students to suggest expansion and publication of their autobiographies, Williams was the one who responded at once, indicating that he was already in the process of expanding and editing his PLA autobiography. Motivated by a set of values profoundly anchored in family, religion, and community, Olgen is a man who responds readily to requests for service.

As the director of Christamore House, a successful neighborhood organization, Williams walks the talk, providing leadership by example. As a survivor of Vietnam, heroin

— ix

addiction, divorce, physical injury, and imprisonment, Olgen has walked in the shoes of those he seeks to serve.

In his talk and through his writing, he explicitly and implicitly poses the question, the challenge: "If I have achieved this, given the barriers I faced, what holds you back? Why can not do you not, do the same or more?" While Williams himself is African American and Protestant, the community he serves and speaks with, for, and to also includes people of many other religions and ethnicities—Catholics and Jews and Muslims, Hispanics and Poles and Irish. Although Olgen's autobiographical story is unique, he believes that it has implications for other humans.

Henry Louis Gates Jr. and other scholars of African American literature have identified such autobiographical genres as the slave narrative, the migration narrative, and the spiritual autobiography. All graduates of Martin University read the autobiography of Frederick Douglass, with his account of progress toward freedom through literacy. Reaching further back in Williams's ethnically specific tradition, Olgen's life and story echo the *Confessions* of St. Augustine, who also transformed his life after an adventurous and profligate youth.

In the end, however, *Healing the Heart, Healing the 'Hood* stands distinct as the story of the unique life of a singular person. As individual as he is, Williams is deeply rooted not only in the historical experience of humanity as a whole but also in the specific history of his community and ethnic group. When scholars and citizens of the next centuries seek to know what life in this turn-of-the-millennium time was like, they will do well to turn to such records in the archive of human experience as Olgen's.

Selene Phillips, in commenting on the distorted pictures of her Native American ancestors in children's books, has raised this challenge: "If you yourself don't write your life story for those readers of the next century, who else will tell your story, and how accurately will they tell it?" *Healing the Heart, Healing the 'Hood* is one response to Phillips's challenge that is a stirring story both for the present moment and for future centuries.

In the particular circumstances of this time, Olgen's balance between God and government, Christ and Caesar, is of special public policy interest. Williams's work in the center he directs, Christamore House, has been identified (and rightly so) as an example of a successful faith-based initiative. Yet Olgen himself is cautiously skeptical about the current political rhetoric from both sides.

His ethic of moral values and hard work may win the hearts of conservatives, some of whom may seek to downplay the need for even partial public funding of community projects or to emphasize morality rather than money as the source of change. Olgen's deft combination of public and private funds and initiatives may appeal to many liberals, some of whom may highlight Williams's projects as effective outcomes of public funding or identify structural socio-economic causes of urban problems.

Yet Williams will frustrate extremists from either side. On one hand, he stands up for the need for continued if not increased public funding of community-based initiatives. At the same time, Olgen invites businesses to re-invest in the urban core and challenges his neighbors to personally commit to neighborhood improvement and, if needed, moral self-reform.

Williams draws a parallel between his personal revitalization and the renewal of the neighborhood in which he lives. As the physical and social environment improves, he believes, so will the lives and conduct of the neighborhood's residents.

Olgen cites the example of Concord Village, a multi-unit single-family public housing development built with 30 million dollars of Hope VI funds from HUD. The extremely attractive, well-built units provide an incentive for families and individuals to adhere to community standards, to maintain the quality of the neighborhood, and to anticipate the possibility of home ownership.

The once-declining neighborhood, thanks to the federal investment in the successful Concord Village project, now has a solid foundation for sustained revitalization. Building upon that base, Williams would like to see similar projects constructed with a combination of government funding and private investment, serving a blend of low-income and higher income residents.

Public funding is also essential to maintain community infrastructure in such areas as schools and libraries, police and fire protection, utilities and roads, health and outdoor recreation. Faith, yes, but not faith alone, will maintain and build community.

For Williams, the role of faith at the personal level is crucial. He recounts his extraordinary experience of a spontaneous healing from heroin addiction as a result of a religious experience within a supportive community environment. More than a half century ago, the Swiss psychologist Carl Jung observed that few patients experienced complete psychological healing without religious belief of some variety.

Olgen's experience not only reinforces Jung's observations but also supports those who suggest that involvement of a "higher power" is an essential factor in addictions rehabilitation. Yet Williams would frame the avenue to healing as a matter of individual choice, a choice that might be encouraged by divine or state intervention but ultimately is dependent upon the individual human's initiative.

Olgen was invited by co-workers to the religious celebration where he was spontaneously healed. Others had prayed for him, but at the moment of readiness it was Olgen himself who chose to come, and his reward was healing.

The challenge of addictions for public policy is not only to broadly provide opportunities for treatment as an alternative to imprisonment but also to nurture environments in which individuals will choose to partake of the opportunities for healing. Faith is a factor, as well as economic opportunity and nondiscrimination, health care and genetic history, family relationships and community support, and education and culture.

Healing the Heart, Healing the 'Hood transcends the stereotypical image of the African-American autobiography, whose writers, as Roland Williams Jr. argues, often represent the most fundamental mainstream American values. Olgen believes in the American dream, as Frederick Douglass did, as

Benjamin Franklin did, in which individuals and community interests converge to serve higher ends and ideals, in which education will lead to advancement, and in which rewards are dependent not upon ancestry or class but upon achievement and integrity.

—Clifford Peterson
September 2004

Westside Community Prayer

Kind and gracious God, we pray
For your blessings on our Westside community.
Make us folks of reconciliation.
In whatever place there is injustice let us
Bring equality.
In whatever place there is mistreatment,
Dignified behavior.
In whatever place there is division,
Unity
In whatever place there is corruption,
Fair play.
In whatever place there is conflict,
Resolution.
In whatever place there is violence,
Peace.
In whatever place there is incapacity,
Power.

Holy Spirit, grant that we may not so much look
To oppose as to collaborate,
To exclude as to include,
To rule another as to serve one another.

Acknowledgments

Special thanks to Dr. Clifford "Skif" Peterson, who encouraged me to complete and to publish this book. Both he and his wife, Lisa Lee Peterson, have given their time and resources to make this book happen. I cannot thank them enough. Diana Etindi, a very good friend, edited my first draft and pushed me to go ahead. Lesia Bostick typed and edited my additions. Sister Michelle Burnett typed the original draft that I wrote in Dr. Peterson's Prior Learning Assessment (PLA) program at Martin University. And thanks to all the people who are praying for my family and me.

Healing the Heart
Healing the 'Hood

My Childhood

When I look back over my life, I sometimes wonder why I am so blessed. I guess it all started back in a little cotton-growing town in western Tennessee called Milan. There I was born on September 14, 1948, to Jimmy Irene Webb and Mike Williams. I was their first child—the first and only son born to the family. In a couple years there was a daughter born into the family, Mackelene Williams; and a few years later there was another daughter born, but she died at birth. One of the things I liked from childhood on was my name—Olgen; it was special, and I took pride in it. My mother chose it just because she liked the name, not because I was named after someone else. I always thought of it as being unique and thought maybe I would grow up to be unique, too.

As I think about my childhood in Tennessee, I feel it was rich. I lived in a family that cared. My mother was a provider. My father was a provider, too, but I did not see him very often. We lived in the time of Jim Crow. Black people were not able to secure skilled trades in the South, so my father, who was a cement mason, had to go to the North to work and send the money back home. My father was Louisiana-born, with straight black hair. He looked almost white. He was a short man, about five-foot-ten, a strong and stocky person with a very volatile temper. But, other than his temper, he was a good man. One of the things I remember about my father most was that when he did come home, he brought a little more discipline to the house.

I remember a few times that I got in trouble for not being truthful.

One particular incident caused me to have real pride in my father. We had a white neighbor, and that neighbor was fussing at my father one day about a tree limb that was blocking his view of the train station. Rather than submissively cowering, backing down, and giving in to the man, my father argued with him and told him what he was going to do if he didn't leave him alone. Right then, my father stood ten-feet tall in my eyes. From that point on, I felt that you could always be a person no matter what color you are, and I always lived my life accordingly. Through my teenage years and adult life, I always dealt with situations from that point of view.

I never had a problem with self-esteem or self-motivation. I have always felt good about who I am, where I came from, and where I was going. My dad put some pride in me as young person, and he was a good role model. I didn't see him often, but when he was around, he was a strong figure for me.

Another thing I recall about my childhood is that I had good birthdays—Davy Crockett suits and new bicycles. I remember my first bicycle. My dad bought it for me; it was a Western Flyer and had the horn built in; it was orange and bright, and I rode it home. I was a happy guy. It was a good life. Because of my dad's skills, we were able to get things that lots of people weren't able to acquire.

Besides my sister and me, my mother raised three of my cousins, too, after her sister died; they were all girls. They got through school and moved away from the house and up north to Indianapolis. My mother was a beautician by trade. When I was four or five years old, I used to go to the beauty school with her down in Humboldt, Tennessee, traveling about thirteen miles each way down the highways. After she successfully finished her training, we opened a shop in our home. Her income, too, afforded us an opportunity to get a lot of material things that many people weren't able to acquire in the South. My parents owned their own home. We lived on the side of the tracks where the somewhat more affluent people lived. My parents' friends were professional people—school teachers and principals.

I liked "the other side of the tracks" when I was little. The people were not as fortunate, but I had fun with them. I used to go over to my friends' houses and eat beans with them and have a good time. Sometimes we would go swimming in the old mud hole out in the country. We stripped buck naked and just swam in that old dirty muddy water. We didn't need much then to have a good time.

In the summer, my friends and their families used to go pick cotton, and I went with them when I was young because my cousin went. I used to pick a little bit, maybe a hundred pounds in a day. The truck would come by, and we'd get on the back of the pickup early in the morning at 5:30 and go into a dewy patch of cotton and start picking. I can remember those cotton patches . . . just as white . . . and some of the cotton so tall it was over my head . . . and the sun beaming down . . . and some of those lies I told. . . . I used to get so hot and lazy that I wanted to go home, so once in a while I faked a headache and the foreman would get mad at me. It was like a summer job to some of the high school kids, but it was a regular job to some of the adults. The wages were pretty poor. I think the best thing I liked about picking cotton is that I could go get some cloth-wrapped bologna and a Hostess cupcake and an RC cola and have a nice lunch. I spent all my money buying lunch, as a matter of fact.

Milan, Tennessee, was a small, quiet town, and it was segregated. Jim Crow was there, but it seemed that it didn't bother us too much; it was just a way of living. I can remember coloreds-only fountains and coloreds-only rest rooms. In the movie theater, we had to go upstairs to the balcony while whites went downstairs, and we had to go outside to purchase our popcorn and candy. I guess in some ways it was considered acceptable then.

Milan used to have great basketball teams. They often went to the state championships—from a little town of seven thousand people—and played the famous Pearl High in Nashville. We lost, but we had the trophies for second place and pictures from the semi-state games. It was a rich history.

I can remember all my grade-school teachers from grades one through six. My first teacher was Mrs. Clark. She was old, but she was a good teacher and kindhearted. One thing I remember most is that she came to my birthday party; we had a big old chocolate cake, and we had fun and played.

Back in those days teachers had a way of dealing with children; they had some strict discipline. We didn't have children who were "hyperactive." If we were, we got in control real quick after a little paddling in the coat closet. We sat straight in our seats and listened, and we learned what we were supposed to. We had a segregated school system in that era, and whatever materials we had were all handed down to us from the white schools. The teachers, though, were dedicated, very intelligent, and educated. They instilled in us a desire to try to get our education and to do the best we possibly could.

I got through those years of Jim Crowism, but my father died when he was fifty-three. I was nine years old when my father passed away, and I can remember how he got sick and found out he had cancer. Back in those days, blacks didn't go to the hospital a whole lot, but they did have a doctor. My father was bedridden at the house. My mother was an excellent nurse, and she nurtured him and cared for him. I can remember him in bed; I used to rub his toes with rubbing alcohol to give him some relief.

The night my father died, I was in the room, and I saw him pass away from this life. It was a sad and a hard thing for me. I can remember the family gathering together at the funeral and the wake from all over the country, from as far as Scotlandville, Louisiana. Not only was it a sad experience but also it was a bitter experience, because my father's family, for some reason, thought that my father had some money and that they should get some of it. They mistreated my mother during that time, and from that point on, I never had any dealings with my father's family. They never called or inquired about the family to see how we were doing. Back in those days, when someone died, the whole town would come out and bring food for the family, the guests, and the relatives. I can remember them eating all that food up and taking all the Cokes away from the house. I learned to get along in life without them.

My mother continued in her profession. Eventually, being a single woman, a widow, she picked up a boyfriend, named Curtis Taylor. Curtis was a good man, tall and slim. He had a reputation of being a bootlegger, a player, and a gambler. He was like a hero, back in those days, from a little town of Trenton, Tennessee. He was kindhearted—until he started drinking. When he was sober, he would give you anything you wanted. When he started drinking, he became abusive, and he abused my mother physically. I can remember coming home and finding my mother with her eyes blackened and her jaw swollen because he had jumped on her. He never did abuse me or my sister or treat us badly, but he constantly abused my mother physically and would cause her lots of mental and physical stress. She accepted it for whatever reason—who knows, maybe she really loved him. She stayed with him, and she went through that for several years.

What finally brought about a change was pretty drastic. My sister, my mother, and my cousin went to visit my first cousin in Fort Campbell, Kentucky. When we came back, the house was burned down to the ground, and we had no place to go. We first thought that Curtis had burned up in there— that he had probably gotten drunk, left a cigarette someplace, and died in the fire. But we found out he was all right. We had to move to another place across the tracks, and my mother had to open up her shop again. Then one day when I came home, her eye was real swollen and bloody; he had jumped on her again. Being an eleven-year-old boy, I was bothered quite a bit, and I can remember I told my mother that if he ever did it again, I was going to kill him.

Because of that statement, she decided to pack up and move. The thing that made me think I could kill him was that Curtis had taught me how to shoot a gun. He had a twenty-two caliber pistol and had taken me out in the yard before and taught me how to shoot it—like a father teaching a boy a man-thing. But that day I had made up my mind that if he ever touched my mother again, I was going to kill him. For my safety, my mother packed up her bags, and she and my sister and I took our little box of chicken and got on the Greyhound bus and sat in the back and rode to the city of Indianapolis.

Growing Up in Nap Town

My cousins were already in Nap Town (as Indianapolis was commonly called then, because there didn't seem to be much going on); so when we got here, we stayed with them. Because my father had worked, we had a Social Security check coming in. My mother secured a place to rent on 30th and Rader. My sister and I started going to School #41, and it was good. Even though she didn't have a license, my mother started doing hair once again; with a Social Security check and her doing a little hair here and there, we made it pretty well. My mother made friends, and she found another "significant other," a good man by the name of Thomas Brown. He wasn't abusive, and their relationship went on for years.

At School #41, I did my thing as an eighth grader and graduated to go on to high school. At that point, I had to go to either Crispus Attucks or Shortridge. I remember a white woman counselor told me I couldn't go to Shortridge; I had to go to Attucks because that's where most black kids went. I said, "All right; no problem." That's just the way things were then, so you didn't think much about it. At that time Shortridge was a college preparatory school with a great reputation, but I went to Attucks, with most of my friends, and decided it was a great school also. It had excellent teachers and an outstanding reputation in sports. Lots of our African American leaders came out of that school.

During the first semester, I was a good student with high grades. One day, however, I found out that their attendance system didn't work too well; I realized I could cut classes and nothing would happen to me. The officials wouldn't know whether I was there or not, so I started cutting classes in the second semester. My grades plummeted, but I was going along quite well on my new schedule—until the school mailed my report card home: I had four F's and one D in the first grading period of the second semester.

My mother had a fit. In fact, she had three fits. She really bore down on me and made me rethink my attitude about school. I went back determined to go to class and to work hard once again. However, at Christmas that year, I got a nice brand-new coat; it was a sharp one, a trench coat. My first week back at school, someone stole it out of my locker. That sealed my fate at Attucks.

My mother said, "You are getting out of this school." She marched me right over to Shortridge, and she told the counselor that she wanted to enroll me in my sophomore year. He looked at my grades and said, "Whoops, I don't know." Then he looked at my first-semester grades and said, "I see you did real good here. What happened?" I told him honestly what had happened, about skipping class and not getting caught. So they allowed me to transfer to Shortridge and finish out my three years of high school there. I didn't like high school at all, though. I wasn't part of one of the in-crowds. I had my group I hung around with, but they weren't exactly the overachievers. School just didn't appeal to me; all I wanted to do was get out. I would have quit, but our teachers kept hammering home the saying, "You need a high school education to get a good job." I believed them, so I didn't quit. However, I just fooled around there, so my grade ranking dropped so low you had to look awfully hard to find it. It's way down there. But that was my fault; I didn't apply myself.

I remember flunking geometry, because a white friend of mine and I slept in class. Somehow, they put me in one of the geometry classes with all the A students. I don't know how I got in there, but it was an accident. I couldn't keep up, so instead of trying to learn right angles and forty-five degree angles, I flunked the course. I got in a whole lot of trouble at home for that. But the classes I liked I excelled in. For instance, I became an A student in history. I really loved that subject . . . and Mrs. Walker, my history teacher. She was an older African American lady, and she really cared about her students and encouraged us to learn. In the classes I liked, I got A's or B's; but if I didn't care for the course, I just barely made it through with a C most of the time.

I wasn't a loner at school. I went out for wrestling. My friends John Bush and George O'Neal were in wrestling. They told me to go out for wrestling, so I did. Come to find out, I was pretty good at it. The school's heavyweight there was Clarence Price, and he was good. He was state champion potential, and I used to wrestle with him. I found out I had kind of a knack for the sport. I could handle all the guys who were 185 pounds, the heavyweights.

I could handle them pretty well considering that I didn't know what I was doing. Not knowing anything, I was doing my little flip-flop and other stuff on them. When the coach saw my potential, though, he got excited.

Participating in a team sport might have made a difference in the way I felt about school, but something happened to change that. As I said earlier, I loved history, and I liked Indiana history especially. I was doing all of my school work and keeping up with my assignments until we were told we had go to a small town in Indiana to do a report; that report became a stumbling block. My mother didn't have a car to take me, and I didn't think to ask anyone in my class if I could go with them, so I didn't turn my report in. That meant I automatically flunked Indiana history. The rest of my grades were all B's or C's, but because I flunked Indiana history, I flunked out of the wrestling team. My wrestling coach was really upset with me and even stopped speaking to me. Eventually, though, we both got over it, and I just went on with school.

At that time, Shortridge had an "English Five" test that students had to take in order to be classified as a senior. It included all the grammar from your junior year back that you were supposed to know. I took the English Five test and did my normal thing—I flunked it. But I didn't feel too bad about that; lots of folks flunked it. Some people took it five or six times. I passed on my second try. I went on to my senior year, did my thing, began to make more friends, began to party a little bit more, and had a drink or two once in a while for fun.

During high school I had crushes on several girls. I fell in love with a young girl by the name of Linda. I thought that by far she was the finest girl at Shortridge. She was the prettiest girl I had ever seen who wore eyeglasses. Her personality drew me even closer to her. I just loved talking to her, and I hoped she liked me back . . . but she liked one of the basketball players. On several occasions when I walked her back home and carried her books and talked, I could have told her how much I liked her, but I never did.

There was another young lady by the name of Shelly. She was bright and very nice looking. Her long pony tail would sway back and forth every time she would walk. My friend Terrell introduced me to her. Her family was very affluent, and their house was huge. She attended a private school, so the only time I would see her was when I would hang out with Terrell in his neighborhood. I knew, deep down, that we would never be a couple, because of our "social differences." I wrote her several letters after I joined the army, and she never wrote back. My heart was broken for the first time. After that, I never wrote to another lady while I was in the army.

I finally got out of high school, having learned a few things along the way. I wish I had learned more. People told me, "You should have paid attention." I realized that too late.

From Nap Town to Vietnam

After high school, Bill Milton, who was a friend of mine, and I made the decision to join the Armed Forces. We went down to the local recruiter and decided to go into the U.S. Army. In October 1966, we joined the Army on the buddy system. We were given physicals and then shipped out to Fort Leonard Wood, Missouri, for basic training. After three years, we were going to be communication center specialists: telephone operators and clerks. On our way, we met Charles Sanders, who had played football for Tech High School and was a great athlete. We became friends on the bus and were put in the same basic training company. We spent October and November in "Little Korea," as they called Fort Leonard Wood. It was cold. Getting up early at four o'clock in the morning and running a mile in zero-degree weather was pretty tough. Trying to bivouac in such frigid weather got so bad, as a matter of fact, that they had to stop us from camping out in tents; people were getting colds, flu, and even pneumonia.

That was an interesting time for us. We were away from home for the first time in our lives. I did fairly well. I was heavy—a little overweight—so they made me a road guard.

They gave me the privilege of running in front of the company and stopping the traffic, so I had to run a little bit more than everyone else. I did a good job, and I lost some pounds. I could do everything we were supposed to do except for the monkey bars, so I got through okay. We got in a few fights while we were there; I guess we were mostly showing off our manliness. Bill was just the kind of guy who got into scrapes and, being his best friend, I wasn't going to let him fight alone. But we all survived, and I actually did really well in basic training. At graduation I was promoted from E-1 to E-2, which served as a little tribute to my success.

We went home on leave and walked around in our uniforms for a few weeks and eventually got bored. The next duty station was in Augusta, Georgia, where we were sent to do our signal training. Bill, Charles, and I all three went down there. That was the first time in my life I had flown in an airplane. I had to fly down to Atlanta and from there go down to Augusta by bus. In Augusta, we lived in old barracks. The first few weeks were pretty simple and easy. We learned to teletype, keyboard, and how to type. The next part was the cryptographic part, and there were two phases of it. It was during the second phase that Bill and I split up. He went to one company and I went to another. Even though Charles "Chick" Sanders was also sent to Augusta, he was in a different outfit. We never understood why Chick wanted to go into mortars in the infantry, but he was kind of gung-ho about the whole thing, so that's where he went. I guess we were a little wimpy, so we went into the Signal Corps.

After Bill and I got separated, I was really on my own—no friends from home. I met a few guys who seemed to be all right, so we used to go into town to the local bars. There was a lot of prejudice and bigotry in the South. I remember going to restaurants in our uniforms, but even in uniform, we still couldn't get served. We didn't think too much of it at that time, because there were enough black bars and restaurants to satisfy the need. But for some reason, I started getting mean and bitter at that same time. Maybe all of the prejudice and bigotry that I usually accepted had somehow seeped into my innermost being and had begun to convince me not to take such treatment anymore.

One time, I started a fight with a white guy and broke his jaw because he was cutting in the line. I didn't know why I acted that way. I really wasn't a very tough guy, but I seemed to be getting mean at the old age of nineteen; maybe I just felt lonely and didn't know how to handle it. At the same time, though, as the Civil Rights Movement progressed, I was becoming more aware of racism and recognizing the injustice of it. I think it started eating at me even before I identified what was bothering me. In one altercation, I smacked my acting platoon leader for calling me "Boy," and got some minor disciplinary action for that.

I graduated from signal corps school as a teletype operator and cryptographic clerk with a secret clearance. I got fortunate and was sent to Fort Knox, Kentucky, right outside of Louisville. It was just two hours away from home, so I could go home a bit more often. There I was assigned to a communication center, where both civilians and military were working. It was interesting at first, and I did my job well but soon got bored. I went to Louisville quite often, went home frequently, and did what soldiers do: I drank a little bit and started smoking Marlboros. Eventually I became so bored and frustrated that I went down to the personnel department and told them I wanted to be put on levy for Vietnam. To my surprise, they said, "Don't worry about it. You're already on levy." I was shipping out in September, going to Vietnam.

I got leave to go home to say good-bye to my friends and mother. My sister had married young and already moved away and started her own family, so I couldn't bid her farewell. The closer it came to time to go to Oakland, California, from where I would fly out to Vietnam, the more I realized that I really didn't want to go. As it turned out, I didn't have money for the ticket to Oakland when it was time to go and ended up getting there three days late. Finally, however, I got to Oakland, waited around a few days, and then was shipped out. It was a long flight—seventeen hours—we stopped for a few minutes in Hawaii, then flew on to Vietnam.

I can remember landing in South Vietnam, where we did our normal military routine. We took our bags, got our assignments, and got a place to lay our heads. That first night was pretty frightening. I could hear artillery firing at a distance and could see the flashing of the guns. Frankly, I was kind of scared. The next day we did our military check-in and all our routines. I got to see my first Vietnamese. It wasn't a good experience. I was an arrogant American soldier, and a male chauvinist to boot.

A Vietnamese woman and I got into a bit of an argument, both of us hurling insults at each other. It was my fault basically; soldiers are not the best people in the world in an occupied country. After about a week of staying at that check-in point, I was told I would be going to the Americal Division, 23rd Division of the Army and I Corps. If someone had asked me where I Corps and the Americal Division were, I wouldn't have known.

They put me on a helicopter—my first time in a helicopter, no doors—and flew me all the way to the northern part of South Vietnam, to a place called Chu Lai. It was a Marine air base on the China Sea. When I got to Chu Lai, I was assigned to Signal Battalion Americal Division as a communications specialist cryptographic clerk. I checked in, found a place to live in my "hooch" (my hut), and hunkered in for eleven months and twenty-five days.

I had come to save the South Vietnamese from the aggression of the North Vietnamese and Chinese. That's what we were being told and I believed it, so I was there to serve and do my duty as an American soldier. After getting settled in, I was delegated to my assignment at a communication center a few yards from the company site. It was a bunker, a sandbag bunker, full of teletype and communication equipment. We communicated with the whole country and with other centers all across the South Pacific.

I remember the first night I had to pull guard duty in Vietnam. I was assigned to the area around the PX where they brought in food and supplies. That first night, another guy and I stole a whole case of vodka. We left our post to take it to the hooch, and then we went back to guard duty. We could have gotten court martialed for that—all for a few fifths of vodka in a case. When it dawned on me what we had done, I was too scared to even drink it. My buddy drank that whole case of vodka by himself. Drinking was common there, though. Sometimes you felt that you had to drink or smoke dope just to forget about your situation for a while. One friend whom I made the first week, a brother named Wilburn, hit the compound drunk and stayed drunk until the last day I saw him.

I made other friends, too—one brother by the name of Little from St. Louis, Missouri, and an older brother named Tibbs from Omaha, Nebraska. He had been in the Army for a while. We called him a "lifer," but he was an E-4; he had been busted down several times. There was a brother named Ray from Gary, Indiana, who acted strange; we were all suspicious of him. It was quite a group of buddies I was surrounded by.

One night they took me down to the Anthem Theater in Chu Lai, where there were little USO shows for the GIs. I got my first introduction to "Mary Jane." I wasn't naive. I knew what was going to happen, but I was with the fellas.... So, I took a couple hits off that joint. That was the first time in my life I had ever used any kind of dope, and I really got high. When I left the Anthem Theater, I was crawling on my knees trying to get out of there, and they were laughing at me. From that day on, I think I got high off marijuana and drank beer every day I was in Vietnam. Eleven months and twenty-five days. That was our daily experience—rolling joints, getting high, drinking, and "rapping" to one another.

Fortunately, I happened to be a pretty good teletype operator, communications center specialist, and cryptographic clerk. I learned the job quickly—how to operate the equipment, how to decode it, and how to set it up. Sergeant Daugherty, a short little white E-6 who was a really nice guy, was over our unit. I worked the night trick: twelve hours— 6:00 P.M. to 6:00 A.M. After a few months, I was promoted to E-4 and put in charge of the night trick, where I supervised about ten guys. We operated the complete message center for the entire compound of the whole Army 23rd Division, Chu Lai. I didn't do much. I was a troubleshooter for the crypto equipment. We would get top-secret messages coming through concerning the activities in Vietnam, and I began to get a different perspective of the war and how it was going.

After work each day and after our four hours' worth of details—filling sand bags, cleaning up for the First Sergeant, or whatever else—we always wanted to go to the village of Chu Lai. That's where the party was. The beer, the prostitutes, the dope. We would get high and do our little partying for a few hours. At 11:30, though, they ran all the GIs out of town, and then later the Vietcong went in and did the same thing we did with the same people. There was a kind of a mutual understanding that this is how it was going to work in that area. It made us wonder what the war was all about and why we were there.

One of the other puzzling things I found in Vietnam is the amount of racism I experienced in Chu Lai. The Vietcong were trying to kill us by throwing mortars and rockets at us every night, but it was men in our own ranks who hated us as well. We had a very serious racial problem in my battalion. What was happening there was a smaller version of what was happening at home in America. In the mid-'60s, the Civil Rights Movement was in full swing. We heard about cities burning and riots taking place in American urban areas. African Americans were rioting. The brothers used to hang out together and talk.

We felt that we needed to be part of what was happening on the home front with the brothers—fighting for the rights of our people. We used to just congregate together. A few white guys would hang out with us and one Hispanic of Mexican descent, Perez, a short man from Texas who used to get loaded every day and then want to fight with white guys. The racial sentiments were so strong that it took very little to ignite a conflict. We used to go to the EM Club, the club for enlisted men—Perez, a brother named Gary, and I. The two of them would always get loaded and want to start a fight, and I joined in, too. I can remember having one confrontation after another.

One time on the way back to the company we had a mini race riot right in the motor pool—some fighting with sticks and clubs. I threw a beer can and hit a guy. The situation really got out of hand. The MPs who were called out locked and loaded on us. In other words, they put ammunition in their guns and told us to halt. I got caught with a metal pipe in my hand. But I was a pretty good liar at that time. I lied to the lieutenant, and one of the acting sergeants who saw me came and lied for me, too, so they gave me my ID and I got out.

That next day, however, the lieutenant colone
Little, Wilburn, and me into his office. The general I
him that if this ever happened again, he was going to be shipped
out. He had heard the word was out that we were going to kill
a white cook who had called us all a derogatory name that
night. There had been talk of getting him, but we found out
he was Hawaiian, so since he wasn't Caucasian, we let it drop.

The racial thing continued to get worse. As new draft-
ees came in with updates about how things were going at
home, our anger towards whites became even more intense.
Perez and Wilburn were really upset. They busted some heads
one night with a bag of ammo clips. They would start fights
with white guys, but then we all had to get in on it. One night
Tibbs busted a guy in the head with a stick. The guy was bleed-
ing all over the place, and we had to run because the MPs
were looking for us. It got so bad that our weapons were taken
away from us on the compound; we were told we couldn't have
them because we were dangerous.

It seemed that we were fighting all the time. You would
think that we could get along in a war situation, but racism
was just too prevalent there. After one particularly bad night
of fighting, we were called out in formation the next morning,
and Little and I were told we were leaving the 523rd Signal
Battalion: I was going to the 196th Light Infantry, and Little
was going to the 198th Light Infantry. They split several of us
up—told us to "pack our bags and get out of Dodge." Little and
I were thought to be the instigators and leaders of the particular
situation there. I didn't think I was so much of a leader, just
one of the guys hanging out.

From Chu Lai I was transferred to Landing Zone (LZ) Baldy Headquarters for the 196th Light Infantry Division. It was in the wilderness. We didn't have a whole lot of luxuries. There I was a communications center specialist and, because of my previous supervisory experience, became the second in charge in LZ Baldy under Sergeant Rayfield, a white guy who was married to an African American woman. We partied together, drank beer, got high together, and even went to Bangkok, Thailand, together on R&R.

LZ Baldy was an interesting experience. I met some brothers from various places. They were a little different from the ones I left at Chu Lai, even a little more radical. One brother by the name of Bladswell from Arizona used to fly the Star and Crest, a flag that typically represents Islam. We sat around and did a whole lot of rapping about the world and the riots that were going on in America, and we listened to the radio to hear whose city was having a riot then. If our city wasn't mentioned, we felt bad. I remember the time Indianapolis had a little thing down on Indiana Avenue—a little burning and a little riot—it made me feel really good that Nap Town was trying to get into the cause for the liberation of the black people in America. That caused me to have my chest stuck out when I was there.

My Meaningless Existence

In September 1968, after eleven months and twenty-five days in South Vietnam protecting Americans from aggression, I came home. But I was a totally different individual from the young man who went there. My views of world politics and America were turned a little differently. And the most significant change in my life was the fact I had been introduced to the drug culture, through marijuana.

Back in the United States, I still had a year left in the military service. I was stationed in Fort Lewis, Washington, right outside the city of Tacoma, a few miles down the highway from Seattle. Stateside duty was miserable; it was a lot more strict, and we didn't do anything meaningful—we cleaned and shined our shoes, went to the field and practiced a little bit, walked guard duty, did KP in the kitchen, and then went out on the weekend to get high and party, spending what little money we had. While at Fort Lewis, I often went down to Seattle, where I got introduced to another kind of drug— LSD. I began to "drop acid," as we called it, and took hallucinogenic trips.

I also got introduced to a different kind of people—people we called hippies. So, my last year in the military consisted of a mixture of militancy, drugs, and the hippies' "free love" philosophy. While at Fort Lewis, Washington, I got a chance to try to qualify to go to the Edgewood, Maryland, proving grounds on a temporary duty assignment. All of us who wanted to go had to meet at a theater one day, where we took a battery of tests to see who would qualify. They picked me to go, and I saw it just as a good chance to get away from Fort Lewis and do something different. When we got to the Edgewood proving grounds, we met people from other forts all over the country. It was only then that we found out what we were doing: we had volunteered to be guinea pigs. We had been selected for an experiment to test various remedies to counter nerve gas. We were never sure just what was being done to us; our food was monitored, and we were tested in chemical warfare suits. Some of the guys were even given hallucinogenic drugs as part of the testing. The day a man first walked on the moon, some of the brothers were in the hospital where they had been given drugs. They told me how they were tripping out and how they were seeing things on the moon as they were watching the event on TV.

Until this day, I don't know all they did to me and the others there, but I do believe it may have affected my physical makeup, my health, and some of the problems I have had since. It seems that perhaps even some of the physical problems my children have had might be traced back to what happened to me there. It amazed me that they kept tracking me for years and could find me wherever I went. They sent me letters asking me to fill out surveys about what I was doing, how my health was, if I had any children and what their health was, etc. I was angry at being used that way, so I never did fill the forms out; I ignored them, and finally they left me alone. Since that time, I have heard news reports about harmful experiments that the government has performed on its military personnel, and I continue to wonder exactly what was done to me.

I was discharged in October 1969 and left Fort Lewis, Washington, with the clothes I had on my back and a little money I had saved up. While I was in the military, I had taken a Civil Service course and two tests to qualify to work in the U.S. Post Office. With my 5-point rating from the service, I got scores of 98 + 5 and 94 + 5, so I was pretty high on the hiring list. Since the draft was going on and people were prospering because of the war, the post office needed people, so they had sent me a letter telling me that I had a job when I got home. But who wanted to work? I had decided that all I wanted to do was just take it easy. I had come to the point that I disdained the military, and even America. I didn't want anything that would remind me of the Army, not even the uniform of the U.S. Post Office.

I got on the plane and flew back to Indianapolis. I went home and stayed with my mother for a little while. I couldn't stay long, however, because of my lifestyle: I spent my time getting high on drugs and partying. After that first thirty days, all my money was gone. At that point, when I was dead broke, I felt I had no choice. In December I became a postal clerk for the U.S. Post Office.

As soon as I got there, I met a young lady with whom I had gone to school. The first thing we did together was to get high. I got to smoking dope again, doing cough syrup and LSD—you name it, I did it.

Coming to work high, I made some more friends. One brother by the name of Denny, another named Steve, and I were into the African American culture thing. Steve had been a pimp before he came to the post office; after one of his girls almost killed a guy, he gave it up and started working a regular job. He was really worldly and wise to the streets; it was Steve who introduced me to heroin, and we snorted it together.

At one point, Steve and I decided to go into the heroin business. I borrowed $500 from a loan company. He went up to Chicago to get a spoon of heroin; we were going to cut it and start our own drug trade. When he couldn't find the right stuff, he took a junkie with him to test it. Instead of coming back with a spoon of heroin, he came back with a stolen 1971 Cadillac Coupe DeVille. He owed somebody a favor, so he bought the stolen car for $500. He pulled up and asked me if I wanted to drive it. I told him I wasn't into Cadillacs and didn't want it. The truth was I didn't really have enough nerve to drive the stolen car. So he gave it to someone else who drove it over to Danville, Illinois, and was arrested with it.

Drugs became my life. My friends and I did heroin and partied every night. Even during breaks at the post office, we got high. Like most drug heads, I thought I could quit any time I wanted to—but who wanted to? I used to do those drugs and go down at night to 30th and Central and stand in front of the Chug-a-Lug, or I'd hang out at 34th and Illinois at Bo's Black Market. Then my buddies and I went down to an apartment in a house at 28th and Delaware, where they would get the water pipe out and we would smoke; some would shoot up with the needle. That's all we did. I had bought my first car—a 1970 Chevrolet Vega, a little old blue thing. So we rode around and partied, rode around and partied. But that lifestyle has a way of eventually catching up with you.

The heroin was really getting to me, and I needed more money, so I started stealing money from the post office. I did this to buy drugs every day. During that time, I also began to get really radical. My friends and I spent a lot of time rapping about what our world was like in the '70s and what we were going to do when the revolution came. We were going to Muslim meetings and having conversations about being the vanguard of the revolution.

We wanted to do something in Indianapolis, and one of the things we wanted to do was to kill some "pigs" (policemen), because they were unjust and treated our people badly. We had nightly meetings to plan our strategy. There were seven of us, and we were getting serious. Each night, we got high and talked about it until eventually we passed out. We knew any night the police could come and take us all to jail (or "the concentration camp," as we called it). Instead, we eventually got busted at the post office; they apprehended me and everyone around me. That broke up our plans.

During that time, I had chased every female who went past me, and finally I began dating Marsha. After I got busted,

I decided to get married, thinking that would keep me out of jail, but it didn't. Having no job while I waited for the court date, I took a few courses at IUPUI (Indiana University-Purdue University at Indianapolis) and went to the Black Student Union. I got disgusted with them, because they weren't radical enough for me. I was blaming the system, the white man, and just about everybody for the situation I was in; I was militant, frustrated, angry, busted, disgusted, and full of drugs.

I finally went to court before a federal judge. I didn't have enough money to get a lawyer, so I had a public defender. He pleaded my case on the basis that I was a veteran; this was my first offense; I had never been in jail, never been arrested, and never even had a speeding ticket in my life. He argued that I had made only that one mistake. But I learned that one mistake was all that it takes. The judge decided that since I had been such a good example but had betrayed the trust that people had in me, he would sentence me to one year in the Federal Correction Institution in Milan, Michigan. That was kind of ironic; I was born in Milan, Tennessee, and now was being sent to Milan, Michigan, to be incarcerated. I remember throwing up the black power salute as I walked away from the judge and down the hallway.

They locked me up in the Marion County Jail. That was a miserable place; it was hot and stinking. Everybody had a story, and everybody was innocent. After two weeks of that, the U.S. Marshals came and took me to Milan, Michigan, to the Federal Correction Institution. That was a place where younger offenders were held, but they had done some heavy crimes—bank robbery and all sorts of federal crimes. When I got there, they put me in isolation. I learned real quick that you had to play this game. I signed up for counseling, a therapy group, to make my record look good. A brother named Grady, also from Nap Town, and I started going to the little therapy group where we yelled at one another, trying to get our heads on straight.

I also started going to the Black Muslims' meetings every Sunday. I started studying with them, reading their paper and the literature, reading Mao's and Castro's writings and anything else I could find on socialism. I used to love those meetings because they used to talk openly about the white man being a blue-eyed devil even while the guards were there listening; we used to "amen" and clap our hands and stomp our feet. We also studied and had good conversation. But for some reason I just didn't believe their doctrine was for me; I didn't think that particular branch of Islam was the proper one. Some of my friends I used to party with at home had become Muslims. They started studying Islam and going their own way. Two of them, John and Jimmy, went west on a Shell credit card, driving a Riviera, to try to "find their destiny in the stars."

In prison, we used to steal Bibles and the Koran to read and try to get our heads on right. I continued playing the game; the counselors wanted me to look good, so I worked out in the weight room (the "iron house," as we called it) and lost a few pounds. The fact is that nothing had really changed. Drugs were available even there, so I still got high. My heart was still wicked, my thoughts were even more wicked. After six months of playing the game, a parole board met and granted me parole. I thought I was just starting my sentence, but they said they were releasing me because I was doing really well. I don't know if that was the reason, or if it was because the place was crowded, or if they just needed to release a certain number. Whatever the reason, it didn't matter to me—I was just glad to get out.

I came back to Nap Town with no job, no where to go. I went back to my wife, but the relationship wasn't good. We had married for all the wrong reasons—she just wanted to be married, and I thought being married might keep me out of jail. Neither of us knew what love was really about; we were both selfish and using each other. Even though we stayed together for a couple of years, it was a time of turmoil and fighting.

Fresh Starts & Old Problems

After two weeks of doing nothing, I finally got a job at Bryant Heating and Cooling, over on Burdsal Parkway, but I lied to get it. There was a question on the application that asked if I'd ever been convicted of a felony. I told them no. I just wasn't going to tell the truth. It didn't seem to matter much anyway; after just a month on that job, I got laid off. But something happened one night during that short time that changed me forever.

I noticed there were some young men on the job there who were a little different from the rest of the crew. They didn't curse; they were quiet and respectful—and they didn't even have Afros, either. I didn't pay any attention to them. I thought they were squares because they didn't have Afros; I thought they were Toms or something. I, on the other hand, was cool. I had my Afro, I kept to myself, and at lunchtime I went out and got high off my hashish. So, as I said, I didn't pay too much attention to them ... or so I thought. The truth is I did pay attention to them. I knew there was a difference.

During this time when I was working at Bryant, I was still radical and kept reading and looking for answers—for something I could really hold on to. I finally came to the conclusion that it must be something spiritual that we needed. While studying black history and learning about the ancient empires of West Africa like Songhai and Mali, I learned how strong those nations were. I realized that there must have been something that kept them together, and I decided on my own that it was something spiritual. So my friends and I started looking for spiritual enlightenment and something higher than us. I didn't want to go to the Black Muslims. I didn't think they had the answer, so we started reading the Koran and looking through orthodox Islam. There we were—seven brothers meeting nightly to rap about overthrowing the city, killing the police, and finding God. During that time, some of the brothers did become Muslim, and some of them went to the Christian faith. And me . . . I was just still looking.

I had a friend named Jimmy. His father was a pastor, and his mother was strong in Christ, and they were praying for us. And Jimmy was changing. I didn't realize at first that he was changing, but it became more and more evident. Jimmy had those roots in him, those things his father planted in him as he raised him up. I went to a Bible class with him, looking and searching. The class was taught by Elder Grier on Alabama Street. I heard him saying how God had blessed Indianapolis, and this and that. I didn't understand what Elder Grier was saying, but I enjoyed what he was saying. And I listened.

Another brother at Bryant was Elder Paul Otis, who worked on the same assembly line I did, putting air conditioners together. He was a man who smiled all the time. I thought there was something wrong with him. But I heard him one day talking to some of the guys about the Holy Spirit, and I started listening. And I said to myself, "The Spirit, Holy Spirit, yeah." As the conversation went on, he asked, "Why don't you come on out to church, and hear and worship with us?" I said, "All right; no problem." At that time, the other brothers and I were looking hard.

I went back to those guys—John, Jimmy, Stanley and the rest of them—and said, "Hey, I talked to this guy and he was talking about the Spirit of God. He asked us to come out to church. Let's go." They said, "All right," so we piled into a couple of cars: three in one car and four in another. We had our dope with us as we drove to church; the car was full of smoke. We were smoking reefers on our way to find God. We had to drive out to the Haughville area of the city to find the church on 11th and Miley. We didn't usually come to Haughville in those days, because it had a reputation; when you went over there across the river, you had to fight back. But I was young, and we were all into it.

We went into that area, but we couldn't find the place. The guys in the other car gave up and drove on down New York Street smoking dope. But we kept on looking. We stopped at a Capitol Oil filling station at 10th and Pershing. An older gentleman pulled up; we rolled the window down, the smoke came rolling out, and we asked him, "Where is New Day Church at 11th and Miley? We're going to find God." And we burst out laughing; he looked at us as if we were crazy.

We finally found the church, and as we pulled up on the lot and heard the music and how they were worshiping and praising God, we got excited.

We said, "This is how people ought to praise God— with some joy and some music." Of course, we were high, we were buttered . . . we were so buttered. And we had some stolen Bibles in our hands, and we had our Afros and wore blue jeans, and I had a beard. We all looked like militants at the time; we played the part. And we were grinning as we walked through the door and down to the front of the church. Some of the members of the church got scared. They didn't know if we had come to cause trouble or what. But we were mild as kittens that night. We sat in the front row, crossed our legs, and went through the service.

Deacon Blaine, a man seventy-something years old, got up and testified about how he had just come off a three-day fast. When I was locked up, I had studied Islam and started fasting and avoiding pork. So what Deacon Blaine said really impressed me. By the end of that service, the effects of the reefer were gone, and we were in our right minds again. They gave a call to discipleship, and something inside of us led John Bush Jr. (Brother Bush, we called him) and me to stand up.

I realize now that it wasn't just "something," it was the Spirit of God drawing us. John and I were baptized that night in the water in the name of the Lord Jesus Christ for the remission of our sins. I didn't understand a lot that night, but I knew something had happened to me, and I felt pretty good about it. Then they asked me if I wanted to receive the Holy Ghost, and I said, "Yeah, but I got to go pick my wife up." I

really didn't know what they were talking about. I told th
though, that I'd come back.

The next night I went back. Even though it was on the weekend, I didn't go to party; I went back to church. I was there, and I was sincere, but I still had dope with me. At one point during the evening, they said, "If you pray through, God will give you the Spirit." I said that sounded good to me. We went back into the prayer room and started praying. As I began to pray, the conviction of God got all over me, and I could see that lid of marijuana, that ounce of marijuana, in the glove compartment of the car. I loved reefers. I smoked those big old joints and I loved that stuff. I was willing to stop doing the synthetic drugs, heroin, and LSD, and thought that would clean my system out.

But I tried to convince myself that marijuana was all right because it was from the ground, it was of nature, an herb God had made; surely there wasn't any problem with that—and, anyway, it would enhance a person's intellect. All those stories commonly went along with dope smoking, to try to justify the action. But that night, as I began to pray, I could see the vision of that stuff in the car, and at that moment I repented and told God that I would be willing to give up anything for Him and to do whatever it took that I might receive His Spirit.

After I had made that confession of repentance before the Lord, God's Spirit entered me, and I could hear myself speaking in a language that I had never learned or even heard before. At the same time, I experienced the joy and the newness of God inside of me. I sensed that a whole new be-

arted; there was a freshness and an inward re-
soul that I had never felt before. When I got
; God, the people around me asked how I felt,
I felt marvelous. I never had an experience
like that in my life. I knew that God had brought peace in my
life and peace in my soul and that I was going to hold on to it.

When we walked out to the parking lot that night
and got in the car, I hit the glove compartment and, taking
out the marijuana, said, "John, I don't need this anymore. I
found what I was looking for." He looked at me in amazement
because he knew how much I loved that stuff. But April 28,
1972, marked a turning point in my life. As I went back to
our friends the next day, they were rolling dope and smoking. I
sat down at the table with them, and they passed me the joint.
I said, "No, I don't need that anymore. I found what we've
been looking for, that spiritual strength." They said, "Yeah,
yeah, all right, brother; that's for you, you know, but yeah, we
ain't ready for that." And from that moment on I stopped going
around them and started serving the Lord Jesus Christ with all
my heart, soul, and body.

Accepting Jesus as Lord and Savior, I soon learned,
gives us a fresh start with God, but it doesn't make life like a
Disneyworld experience where everything is suddenly all beautiful and life is fun and there are no problems. I was still living
in a very real world, and I was living with the results of some
bad decisions I had already made in my life. My marriage, for
instance, did not make a miraculous turnaround; in fact,
things in my home got worse than before.

My wife had gone through a lot. We had met at the post office, where we both were working. She had become pregnant before I was arrested, and she lost our twins while I was in the correctional facility in Michigan. When I got out, I had no job and spent my time hanging out with my friends, just as I had before. Marsha didn't like my friends and naturally wanted me to spend time with her instead of them. Of course, I was still a male chauvinist, and I was still "doing my thing" and looking out for my own interests. My wife had her own issues she was dealing with, and she, too, had begun drinking and hanging out with her friends. We really didn't have a marriage in any true sense of the word.

Oddly enough, when I became a Christian and started living a different lifestyle, my wife started going further in the opposite direction. She went to church with me a couple of times, but she resented my relationship with God and with the church, and she wanted me just to stay home and be with her. Of course, now that I'm older and have grown in knowledge and understanding both of God and of human beings, I can see that I didn't handle things well. I certainly didn't have any "people skills" and knew nothing about how to build a relationship. So I know I failed her, and I feel bad about that. For the period that followed, we had good days and bad days and tried to make the best of the situation, but we were living poles apart in terms of our interests, our lifestyles, and our hopes for the future.

That following year, we had a baby—a beautiful little girl named Kim. I was excited about becoming a father, and I really wanted to take care of this little baby and to protect her and be a good dad to her. Unfortunately, my marriage continued to fall apart. I took care of our daughter while my wife worked, and then she would come home and care for her while I worked. I continued to be involved in my church and always got Kim dressed and fed and took her to church with me; Marsha spent more and more of her time out with her friends.

One night, I was waiting for my wife to come home from work so that I could go to work, but she didn't come home. I was waiting and watching out the window for her, and it was hurting me pretty bad that she hadn't come home. As I kept watching at the window, I finally saw a car pull up in front of our apartment building and then go slowly down the street a little ways. I walked out of the apartment to the car, and there she was—a guy she worked with had brought her home. I went over to the car, opened the door, introduced myself to the man, and said, "How you doin'?" Then I said to her, "Come on; come on home." They acted as if he was just bringing her home from work, but she seemed embarrassed and didn't say much; she just got out of the car and we went into our apartment.

Another time, not long after that, Marsha had driven to work but came home without her car. When I asked her about it, she gave some excuse that really didn't make any sense. Before I went to work, I looked in the phone book for the name of the man who had driven her home before; I found it, drove past his address, and saw her car sitting there just down the street from his house. I walked up and knocked on his door, asked him if he would drive Marsha's car home, and told him

I'd bring him back. He agreed to do that. When we got to our home, I asked them to tell me if there was anything going on that I should know about. They said no, that he was married, and that they were just friends, but again Marsha looked embarrassed. No longer being the same man who would once have beaten up both of them, I simply said okay and took the man home. All the way home, however, I witnessed to him about what God had done in my heart and the difference Jesus had made in my life. (A few years later, that man became a Christian, too.)

Things between my wife and me continued to disintegrate. We were always arguing and fussing, and we grew further and further apart. Things happened as she continued to drink and her personality continued to change, but the end result was that she eventually kicked me out of our home and told me she was going to get a divorce. I told her that I didn't want the divorce, that I wanted us to try to work things out, but she was adamant. During that time and for the next few years as things were said and done, I had to learn how to put things I couldn't handle into God's hands and let Him take care of them. The one thing I'm most thankful for from all of that is that God eventually restored a relationship between my daughter and me. I know she suffered a lot from everything that happened as a result of her parents' problems and decisions, and I deeply regret that, but now we are together often, and we have a close and loving relationship.

Growing Up . . . Again

It wasn't only at home that my fresh start encountered difficulties. After that night at church when God changed my life, I went back to work at Bryant, but I got laid off a few weeks later. They told me that it would only be for a few weeks and that they were going to hire again soon. In a few weeks, I went back in and faced that same application that I had lied on before to get the job. I looked at it, paused, and knew I couldn't lie this time. I had to tell the truth, no matter what it meant. So I marked "yes" that I had been imprisoned, and I then wrote an explanation of my situation. God proved faithful to take care of me when I acted in obedience to Him; I still got the job.

When I went back to Bryant, I had some good brothers there: William L. Harris Sr., who became Bishop Harris, my pastor now; Paul Otis Jr.; Ernest Clay; and Cornelius Bullock—all now pastors. Those brothers, none of them pastoring then, were strong Christians; they lived right and wanted to do right, and they helped me as a baby Christian. When I got put on nights, I was really blessed because all those men were on nights with me. All of us went to the same church, so we worked together and worshiped together.

I had started going to Sunday school and church on the first Sunday after I came to Christ. I first went out to Richmond Brothers and bought myself a green suit because I didn't have any suits. Then I went to church and Sunday school, and I started studying my Bible. Those men from work helped me and nurtured me and brought me along.

I loved books. I went to the library and checked out books and studied. I used to have thirty books at a time from the library. I studied the Sunday school lesson, read the Word of God, went to Bible class, and tried to learn all I could; I studied Hebrew, Greek, homiletics, hermeneutics—anything I could, just like a dry desert trying to soak in life-giving water from an unexpected rainfall.

At work, I witnessed to other men about how Christ changed my life, and the Lord blessed those times. Johnny Hendricks was shooting heroin when God arranged for us to work together and gave me the opportunity to witness to Him. One day at noon time, he went and got baptized and then went home and threw away all his needles. God filled him with the Holy Spirit, and he has served since then as a pastor, an evangelist, and an elder. John Bush got saved a few months after that, and he is now an assistant pastor down in Texas. Those are just two examples. The Lord gave me a power for witnessing, and several young men who worked at Bryant became Christians and eventually went into the ministry.

In 1974, I again got laid off from Bryant. By then, my wife had divorced me, I had child support to pay, I had no income, and things just weren't going well. During that time, though, God gave me new strength and guided my steps. Through the GI Bill, I enrolled in computer programming at Ivy Tech State College, and I earned a little money as a work-study student working in the Veteran Affairs Office. My good friend Bill Milton, who had joined the service with me on the buddy system, was in charge of Veterans Affairs at that time. He was taking care of the veterans' paperwork and signing them up for school; he let me work and help him out in his office, and eventually I was officially given the job of clerical assistant. I did a lot of the paperwork—helping fill out forms for the GIs, typing up business letters, etc. I didn't much know what I was doing, and I couldn't really type, but I learned.

In spite of my efforts, I ran into a few problems. It was in that position that I realized I couldn't work very well with other people in certain situations. I had a hard time getting along with others, and I would bump heads with people once in a while. The supervisor over both Bill and me was a lady named Doris. Being a Christian made me no less a male chauvinist at that time, so Doris and I bumped heads often. I refused to submit to her authority, and she resented the fact that I wouldn't. It wasn't that I didn't do my job; I did what she asked, but I did it with an attitude. Doris was frequently upset with me, so after the first year, they didn't renew my contract. I continued in school, but after a couple years, I realized I didn't want to be a computer programmer, and I didn't want to sit in an office and wear a tie, so I started looking for a job.

At that time, I rented a little place in the 1100- block of Tremont from my barber, Douglas Tate Sr. My mother lived in Tennessee with her boyfriend, Thomas Ed Brown, and they were doing pretty well. They owned a Lincoln, a Cadillac, and a Cutlass. Sometimes, while I was job hunting, they let me borrow one of the cars, so I drove around Haughville in a Lincoln or a Cadillac, wearing a suit every day. People in the neighborhood didn't know what to make of me.

Some of them thought I was with the FBI because of the suits. Some of them thought that I was a homosexual because I wasn't married and they never saw me with any women. They didn't know that I went to a church where we didn't believe in premarital sex or even dating as most people know it, because the Bible doesn't support that kind of activity. I get a good laugh today when I think about the image people had of me then. Pastor Harris has told me that he used to "defend me" when some of my Haughville neighbors began telling stories about me.

Bishop Harris and his wife became my best friends. They kind of watched over me and tutored me, and after the divorce I often used to go over to their house to eat. I was a lonely person during that period; I didn't really have anybody close to me but them. I wasn't close to my family because I was serving the Lord, and they were doing their thing, and we didn't have anything in common. The Harrises took me under their wings and nurtured me, and we had some good times together. Pastor Harris and I worked at Bryant together, got laid off together, and spent our unemployment time together.

He was a good friend and a good example of a strong Christian walking before the Lord. At first, he was my Sunday school teacher in the young adult class at New Day Pentecostal

Church, where I was a faithful participant. Eventually, though, he moved on to teach the adult class; Brother Paul Thomas was chosen to teach the young adults, and I was named as his assistant. Brother Thomas used to let me teach every other Sunday, so for about two years I developed my teaching and preparation skills, and I also developed a desire to one day be a Sunday school superintendent.

In 1976, Bishop Turner, my pastor at New Day, died. Some things started happening there then that the Harrises couldn't agree with. In order to avoid conflict and to keep peace in that church, they simply moved their membership, and I went with them. I left not only because they were my best friends but also because I had a lot of confidence in Elder Harris and saw him as a man of God, a man of strength and character, and I felt I needed to be with people of strength and character. So we went to Emmanuel Temple, under Bishop Nathaniel Madden, out on the 6100-block of Michigan Road. We felt at home there because Bishop Madden believed as we did in the standards of God's holiness and righteousness, and we enjoyed worshiping God there together.

While I was job hunting, a friend named Mike Harper invited me to go with him out to Rock Island Oil Refinery where he said they had jobs for us. He pointed out that I wasn't doing anything anyway, so we hopped in the car and went out to Rock Island on 86th Street. I had vaguely remembered seeing that place because it had a flare that burned constantly to burn off the gases, but I had never really been right there at the refinery before. The place stunk with the smell of petroleum. We got there late in the afternoon, about four o'clock;

Mike went into an office while I stayed in a waiting room. A white Jewish guy and a little black guy named Nate came out of the office. Nate used to work at Bryant and he remembered me. He had been at Rock Island for a while and had been promoted to assistant safety director. His department and the human resources department together accepted the applications. Both Mike and I filled one out; I answered all the questions. They told us they were looking for women right then, but to come back in two weeks and they might be hiring.

Two weeks later, I called back, and I was told to come on out. I interviewed with Norm Rosenburgh and Nate McDonald. Rosenburgh looked at my application and said, "I see here you been convicted of a felony. Would you like to tell me about it?" I told about my past life and how I was into drugs and got incarcerated for stealing at the post office. But I told him, too, that I had since become a born-again Christian and that because of what Christ did in me, I was a different man. I told him, "Since then, I haven't done drugs, haven't done anything illegal, and I'm a new person—I just don't do those things anymore. My whole philosophy of life has changed and I am a person of morals and values because of God's grace." He said that was interesting, and that they would get back to me. When I was leaving the room, I heard him tell Nate, "This is the kind of guy we need—somebody that's up-front and honest." A short time later, they called me and told me I was hired. I started there in October 1977 as a laborer, making seven-something an hour.

I was learning through these years of difficulty that God could take care of me. He could provide people to care for me when I had no one who cared. He would help me through hard times—not because I always deserved His help, but because He always loved me anyway. He taught me not to retaliate, but instead to trust Him to protect and defend me. He taught me that I could keep His commandments and trust Him, despite the consequences that surfaced from my past—even as I told the truth on my job application, admitting to being a former felon, and still got the job.

God taught me about humility and true manliness by putting an example before me to demonstrate those qualities. He showed me through my studies what Jesus was like and put a desire in me to be like Him. I came to realize that April 28, 1972, was just the beginning of a long journey. Day by day, God was helping me to grow up; moment by moment, He was stretching me from childhood to manhood, getting me to the point that He could accomplish His purposes through my life.

Love, Life & Lots to Learn

Earlier the same year that I moved out to Emmanuel Temple, I had written a letter to God, telling Him very simply the things that I really needed at that point in my life. Some of the needs were spiritual, but others were very practical; I believe that God cares about all aspects of our lives. In that letter, I told God that I wanted a closer walk with Him and desired to learn more from His Word. Also, I wrote that I needed a job making $16,000 a year; I needed a car; and I wanted a wife who was going to help me walk with Him and who would be a strength to me and not a hindrance. I had been divorced for about four years, and my former wife had remarried, so I felt free before God to also seek a new marriage partner. I put that letter in my Bible and waited on the Lord.

When I began attending Emmanuel Temple, I saw a sister there named Mary Laster, who had a daughter about ten years old. Mary was slender and attractive, but the main thing I noticed was her sweet and quiet spirit. This woman was very faithful to the church; she was from Muncie, and she used to go back to Muncie on Sunday nights with Bishop Madden to services at a church up there. She was quiet and didn't say a whole lot, but she seemed to be obedient to God and to live her life to please Him. By that time, I was a pretty lonely guy. The Scripture says a man who finds a wife finds a good thing and obtains favor of the Lord, and I felt that it might be God's will for Mary and me to be together.

I started courting Mary, but not in the traditional sense. We believed in letting God guide us and show us whom He wanted us to marry, not in figuring out who we felt most attracted to by holding hands, kissing, petting, and all that. I began to seek God's will about Mary and me. I prayed a lot, fasted a little, and sought counsel from my best friend; He also believed she would be a good wife for me. After a few months, I felt assured in my heart that God wanted us to be married. Even with all that, I was scared to ask Mary; not dating her in the common way, I didn't know definitely how she felt, and I was afraid she would say no. But, much to my joy, she said yes, and we got married about six months later, on June 10, 1978.

After Mary and I got married, we settled down in a little ol' apartment with her daughter, Angie, who was about eleven. At that time, Mary was working at Mayflower, a moving company on 96th Street and Michigan Road. She desired to quit her job so she could be at home for Angie when she got home after school. God had given me a job at Rock Island the year before, so I was making good money and having Mary stay home was not a problem; I was glad to have her at home to greet me also when I got off work. I knew that God had given me a jewel.

We settled in, and we bought things that people normally buy as newlyweds—a few items for the apartment. A little later on, we were able to buy a better car. Before I knew it, God had answered all of the prayers I had included in my letter to Him the year before. Of course, the first request, about having a closer walk with Him, is one that will never be fully answered this side of Heaven. I'll always want to continue to draw closer to Him and to know His Word more fully.

The job at Rock Island continued with me working as a laborer and a janitor, but I desired to move up into other areas of the plant. I also wanted to be able to attend church on Sundays, which my job then prevented. So I prayed hard, and I kept a job as a janitor for two years, until the right job came up, one that would be flexible enough for me to be able to be at church on Sundays. God blessed me with a job at the pump house, and I became a pumper. I learned quite a few things there. Most of those things I can't use in most other jobs because the information dealt specifically with the oil refinery. But I did learn helpful things about the environment, hazardous materials, safety issues, and OSHA rules and regulations. That job went on for several years.

One of the problems with Rock Island at that time was that they didn't have lots of minorities in supervision, only a couple. Two blacks—no females, no Hispanics or any other minority group—had been promoted. There was a little grumbling and mumbling going on. The union at that time was no help, either. They were just as hard on the minorities as the company was when it came to involvement and relations. No union officials were from those ranks either. No one seemed to want to do anything about it because when you're making good money—thirty, forty, fifty thousand dollars or more a year, it's hard to complain about your plight in life.

One of the things I desired, though, was to move on up to supervision because I was tired of the union—not knowing every two or three years if we were going to go on strike, and some of the things they were doing didn't seem right. I was just frustrated. I went to my knees in prayer, and I asked God if perhaps He would help me get moved into supervision. During that same time, a lot of the workers did a lot of mumbling and complaining, and filed grievances, so I thought maybe we could do something about it. I decided to write a letter to the human resources director addressing the issue of the lack of minority promotions and opportunities given to us in the plant.

I had come of age in the '60s and had embraced the radical philosophy of the Black Panthers, and I had called for "power to the people" and was used to making demands and being willing to fight for what I believed in. I still had a little of that spirit in me, but I had mellowed a bit, and I had become wiser and a lot humbler since being born again. So I wrote a letter of consideration to the proper authority and requested a meeting. Before I sent the letter, I went to every minority and to any other person who had been slighted or overlooked by management and asked them to sign the letter. I felt it was important that we get every signature, and we did; even those I thought probably wouldn't sign, did. We sent that letter, and they granted a meeting with me and two of the other workers. We sat down and had a cordial conversation and we expressed our concerns and complaints; as at most places, they didn't promise us anything but said that they appreciated us for bringing issues to their attention and that they would look into the matters.

Initially, we weren't sure of their sincerity, but from that point on, things began to change slowly. We hadn't put them in a corner, and we didn't demand or threaten; we just asked for consideration, and they responded. One thing I had learned is that if we had made a big deal in making demands, the white workers would have gotten upset and offended, thinking that the company was going to do more for minorities than for others at the plant. That would just have made them angry and wanting to retaliate toward us, and it would have put the company in an awkward position, so that no matter what they did, it would have been "wrong." The way it was handled was wiser and more subtle. It was low-key and quiet, but it brought about the desired response. Gradually, changes we recommended were made in the plant, and minorities began to be promoted.

About 1990, Marathon Oil Company came in and bought Rock Island refinery, and then things really did change. We didn't lose any money in our hourly wages, and we didn't lose any benefits, but there was a big change in the way we did business; the whole operation became more professional. Marathon put about sixty million dollars into the plant to bring it up to snuff. At that same time, we got a new supervisor, and he noticed my attitude and the way I did my work, and I was asked if I would be interested in being a foreman in my department. It meant more money, and I wouldn't have to work overtime to make an adequate wage. I went to my wife, and we prayed about it and felt that God was opening this door for me.

I took the job as foreman, and as I worked in that position, they gave me the opportunity to get more training in supervision techniques. I supervised a department of about twenty men and was responsible for coordinating the fire and emergency operations throughout the refinery. Had there been a fire, we would have had to work with the Marion County Sheriff's Department and the Washington and Pike Township Fire Departments to resolve the problem. Fortunately, there were no major emergencies while I was there.

The worst disaster that happened to the company during the period I was employed there was the time someone left a valve open, which allowed oil to move outside the plant and into the creek. The oil went down the creek and into the sewers, and a house several blocks away exploded as a result of the fumes being emitted. Charges were brought against the company, and Marathon was fined a lot of money, had to clean up the mess, and received a lot of negative publicity. Of course, the environmental people were very upset by that incident, so they gave us more environmental and hazardous waste training on how to deal with situations like that.

Marathon built a wastewater treatment plant, where we treated the water from the processing part of the plant. We cleaned it up, taking the oil and the chemicals out of the water, before it was released down to the sanitation sewer. I was the lead person in training my department and other foremen in how to apply the chemicals to the process and how to regulate the pumping operation as well. It provided me a good opportunity to learn about environmental control and to learn the new plantwide computer system that monitored all the tanks, the operations flow, and the pipeline shipments that came into the plant.

The job at Marathon was good, and I enjoyed working with my supervisor, Russ Bunton, and my foreman, Jesse Lowry. We had a good group of guys and didn't have to fire anyone, but the biggest problem we had was keeping guys awake on shift. Since we basically had to be on hand to deal with emergencies, we didn't have work that kept us constantly busy. We had time to read, to eat, and occasionally even to watch ball games.

It was a relaxed job as long as there were no emergencies to handle, and because of the technical expertise necessary, it was financially rewarding. When I left there, I was making about $53,000, so I was blessed. However, before Marathon closed, I had to have cataracts removed from both eyes, and I was diagnosed with diabetes and high blood pressure. I am still dealing with both on a day-to-day basis, and with the help of God I am still able to function at my work.

In June 1993, we got word the plant was closing because it was losing money and it would cost the company $60,000,000 to bring it up to safety standards. In announcing the closure, Marathon offered the supervisors the option of transferring to other refineries in their system. I was given twenty-four hours to decide if I wanted to accept a job at a refinery in Texas. Feeling really settled in Indianapolis, with my wife, children, other family members, and friends all here, I declined the offer.

I was given a second offer. They needed to continue the tank and loading facility operation, and they would retain three people here to handle that work. Two other men in my department and I were offered the jobs. The other two guys signed on to the job right away, but I hesitated, wanting to pray about it. My wife and I talked it over, and I went to my pastor for counseling. After much thought and prayer, it seemed that this was an opportunity for me make a change in my life. Rather than working seven days on alternating shifts, I could take the little bit of money I was being given and put my faith that God would make a way for me to do something else.

For about three years, I had been running a little business on the side, doing some cleanup, light hauling, and grass cutting. It had given me a little extra money and was pretty successful. I thought now I could just invest a little more money and let that occupation grow and become an official business. After the plant closed down and everybody said their goodbyes and went their own ways, I started Maranatha Diversified Services—a light hauling, janitorial, and lawn care business. I bought another truck, some additional equipment, and lawn care tools in order to do the work.

I wanted to do this right, so I took a couple of classes on small business development at the Indiana University Small Business Center. Elaina Looper, one of my former Ivy Tech teachers, was invaluable to me in helping me through the application to become a certified minority business enterprise. It took several months, but I got bonding, insurance, and a general contractor's license. As I began to advertise, new customers called and my business began to grow a little bit. I operated the business until I had an accident and broke both wrists.

The Blessing of Family

I felt sure that God was going to make a way for me because I had a wife and children and it was God's will that I take care of them and feed them. The Bible says that children are a gift, an inheritance from the Lord. It was my responsibility to care for these children God had given me, and I believed He would provide the means for me to do that. God blessed Mary and me with many children—ten, in fact. In addition to my first child, Kim (b. 1973), and my stepdaughter, Angie (b. 1966), we also had six sons and two daughters.

Kim and I were separated for several years, with child support being our only connecting link, but God wonderfully restored that relationship, and we are very close now. Just like her father, Kim made some bad choices earlier in her life, but now she is working hard at a couple of jobs, has gotten her life together, and has become a beautiful woman.

When Mary and I got married, her daughter, Angie, was entering puberty, which is a difficult time of life for everyone. The change in her home life was very hard for her. She was accustomed to having her mother to herself, and, in her mind, I'm sure I was an intruder and infringing upon her relationship with her mother. She also was not used to having a father figure around, and I brought more discipline into her life than she was used to, so it was a hard adjustment for her. She knew deep inside that her mother and I loved her, but as she entered her teen years, she began to rebel against our authority, as teenagers often do, and made many decisions that were not in her best interests. One of the hardest things a parent has to do is to stand by and watch a child make bad choices in spite of all of your prayers, your love, and your counsel. I wish I had known better how to help Angie avoid the pitfalls she encountered, but at times all we could do was help her pick up the pieces after the damage had been done. Thankfully, she never got into drugs or alcohol, but she got hurt a lot from bad relationships. She is a grown woman now and is getting her life back on track. She is married and more settled, and she is revealing more of her true nature now—that of a good and kindhearted woman who watches out for her mother and who wants her own life to have meaning and purpose.

The first child born to Mary and me was our son Olgen Michael (b. 1979). I wanted him to have my name because I was always proud of it, but knowing how hard it has been for people to learn to pronounce it, I wanted him to have the choice of a more common name as well. At first, he went by "Michael," but he learned over the years to like "Olgen" and goes by that now. He has my name but his mother's personality. He is quiet and pleasant. He's built like his mother, too, tall and slim. Like me, he didn't enjoy school or apply himself as he should have, but he graduated from high school and is working two jobs. He thinks he would like to become a fireman, and we hope that works out because he would be very dedicated to his work of helping others. He's always been a good kid and now is becoming a good man.

Joi (b. 1980) was the second child born to Mary and me. Her name expressed the feeling we had when we looked down at her and saw this perfect little baby and began to look forward to seeing her grow up strong and healthy. Being Christians, however, does not keep us from experiencing hard times and troubles that challenge us to the very core of our being. When Joi was just nine months old, she went into seizures which damaged her brain and left her physically impaired and mentally challenged. She was left in a state that will require her to be cared for all of her life; she can't do much at all for herself and still has seizures often, even though she's on medication. We can see, though, how God has used even this situation to teach us what real love is all about and to teach us patience and dependency on Him. Throughout her life, Joi has always done what she could and we love her; in spite of the circumstances, she truly has been a joy to us.

Our next child is our big guy, Jason (b. 1981). So different from his older brother, he is very vocal and outgoing—more prone to fighting than to reasoning things through. He's an intelligent and perceptive guy, very gifted mechanically, who enjoys business. He's working now and going to school at Ivy Tech. He will probably be our first son to get married and will likely settle down and be a businessman some day.

Timothy (b. 1983) is a really active kid; he's had difficulty staying focused at school and concentrating in class. I see so much of myself in Tim—a scary thought when I know all I had to go through on my way to maturity—but we have brought him up with the knowledge of God and have let him know that the most important things in life are living for God and serving others. He doesn't know what he wants to do yet when he's finished with school, but we trust him to make the right decisions and believe God is going to do good things with him. Right now the goal is just to get through school. He started at a Kroger grocery store and got promoted to a cashier's position, so he has proven that he can work hard and accept responsibility.

As Angie was going through some of her turbulent times, she could not care for her daughter, Nicole (b. 1984), so we brought her into our home and, in order to assure that the state would not someday place her somewhere else, we formally adopted her. She is fifteen now. Nicole is facing all of the typical problems of a girl that age, but she has a very sensitive spirit and has big dreams for the future. She is on the honor roll and is capable of doing great things with her life. We're so glad she has been such a part of our life.

One of our greatest tragedies was having another daughter, Rebecca (b. 1984), who was born with a bad heart; we had to decide whether or not to have surgery performed to try to correct that problem. It was one of the hardest decisions we ever had to make, but seeing how tiny and fragile she was and knowing all of the problems she might have even if the heart problem was corrected, we decided not to have the surgery done and just to leave her in God's hands. We knew we could trust Him to make the right decision and that whatever He did would be the right thing. We made it clear that we did not want the operation done. The doctors, however, overrode our decision; they rushed her into the operating room and performed the surgery against our will.

After the operation was over, they came and told us that her heart problem was caused by a chromosome condition. The doctors confessed that they should have caught it before but that they hadn't. They explained that babies with this problem don't live even to be a year old. They also admitted that they should not have operated because it really wasn't going to do any good. She would never be able to respond as a normal baby to our voice or our affection, and they recommended putting her in a facility. Of course, we would not do that; she was our daughter, and she would live with us. Our little Rebecca had to stay in the hospital for two months. After being sent home, she lived until she was four months old, and then she died one day in her crib as I stood and watched her helplessly.

This was such a sad time for Mary and me, and we were angry and upset, too, because of what the doctors had done. It would have been so much easier to have said goodbye to her that first day and to know that she was going right from our arms into Heaven. Instead, we had to watch her tiny body try to recover from radical surgery and to watch her simply lie in her crib and in our arms day after day, knowing she would never get any better; it was heart-wrenching. The final straw was getting a bill from the hospital for $4,000 for the operation. I simply refused to pay it; that was the only way I had of saying, "What you did was wrong." As Christians, we didn't feel we should sue the doctors and hospital or take the situation to the news media, so we just had to give the situation over to God and let Him bring healing to our hearts over the matter.

Even now, I know it has been hard for Mary to let go of the pain brought by the situation. I had to ask God's forgiveness for bitterness and anger I had toward the doctors and, in a sense, toward God for letting our baby be born that way. God knew my feelings were natural, but He didn't want them to eat me up inside and destroy me. This side of Heaven, we'll never understand some of the things we have to go through, but I do know that we have a deeper capacity for compassion for others because of the pain we have experienced ourselves. There's no more loving woman in the world than my wife, Mary.

The doctors told us that Mary shouldn't have any more children because there was a possibility they could be born with the same problem. We never anticipated having a large family anyway, so that would have been okay with us. We do believe, though, that children are a gift from God, so, while we didn't try to make things happen, we weren't going to prevent God from blessing us either, if He chose to do so. We had three more children after that—all born perfectly normal and healthy.

Aaron (b. 1985) was next. He's an interesting guy; he can be an angel or a demon. He's very smart, very intelligent; he can accomplish anything he wants, and he has even won all sorts of awards for various academic achievements. As with a lot of fourteen-year-olds, though, he doesn't always appreciate that his intelligence is a gift from God, something to be used humbly and faithfully for God's purposes. We know, though, that he is in God's hands, and we trust that he will not waste time as I did as a young person but will instead let God use his life to all of its potential. He can grow up to do wonderful things in this world, if he but chooses to do so.

Jonathan (b. 1987), who is just entering his teen years, looks more like me than any of the other children did at that age. He has a great personality and is always smiling. I call him Dennis the Menace because he can be really mischievous at times. If he will just buckle down and apply himself and be willing to work, he could go far in life.

Just as Jonathan and David, according to the Bible, were best friends, our Jonathan and his younger brother, David (b. 1989), are also very close. As the "baby" of the family, David has had a lot to deal with from his older brothers and sisters. He used to be the quietest one in the house, but now he's the loudest. Mary always says that because he's the youngest, he feels as if he has to be loud to make himself heard above everyone else. He is on the honor roll and, along with Jonathan, is a Boy Scout.

Being a father is the hardest job I ever had. It has always been a challenge to me. I know God has placed these children in my care for me to watch over, nurture, educate, and love. I know that they belong to God and He will hold me accountable for seeing that they are well prepared for their adult lives, even though they are responsible for their own choices they make in life. I've taught them to work hard and to be honest. They have never had a lot of material things, because with such a big family, there are always so many needs that you can't afford too many luxuries.

They have learned that there are things more important than wearing brand-name clothes and having the most expensive sneakers. As they get older, they are getting their own jobs and can buy some of the things they really want for themselves. Our kids are really good kids. They each have their struggles, but they have good hearts, they are respectful to their mother and me, and they want to do something with their lives. Their mother and I are very proud of them, and we love and value each one of them, appreciating each individual's uniqueness.

Most of all, I try to be a good example to my children. I try to take them with me whenever I can, so that they will understand what's going on in and outside of the neighborhood and will be able to see how they can find ways to help make the community better. I've always tried to be someone they could be proud of. They have never heard me curse, have never seen me smoke or drink, and have never seen me mistreat their mother.

Even when I went back to school, that was in part to set an example for them and let them know how important it is to get a good education. I hope that they will avoid making the same mistakes I made and won't have to learn things the hard way. I know that whatever they choose to do in life, if they do it in service to God, they will find peace and fulfillment.

I just pray all the time that God will help me to be a good father and a good husband.

One of the greatest blessings of my life is my wonderful wife, Mary, for whom I thank God. I could never have accomplished so much with my life—the involvement at church and in the community—without the support of this great woman. Proverbs 31:10 says, "Who can find a virtuous woman, for her price is far above rubies." That's exactly how I feel about Mary. She is worth more to me than I can put into words. She is a quiet person, easygoing, and so very patient; she puts up with a lot of things from me. I'm sure I don't tell her enough, but I love her so very much. I know that for everything I do in my life, she deserves credit. Without her, it never could have happened.

One incident in particular shows the enormous amount of love and care she has shown to me. In 1995, my business was doing well, and I was also serving as a board member and vice president of WESCO (Westside Cooperative Organization). Life was going just fine for us. One Saturday morning in July, I was volunteering some time to do some work on the new building WESCO was moving into. I climbed on top of a twelve-foot stepladder, getting ready to pull out some old tile. Suddenly, the ladder broke and twisted on me. I was thrown off, flipped around, and, with my hands out in front of me to try to catch myself, I landed hard on the concrete floor. In pain, I tried to get up, but I couldn't. I was rushed to the hospital, where I found out I had broken my right wrist, shattered my left, and gotten a big gash and a small concussion in my head.

The doctors operated on me to repair my wrist, but there went my self-employment. With one arm pinned up, the other in a cast, stitches in my head, and constant pain, I couldn't drive a truck, haul trash, cut grass, or do anything. We had no insurance, no money coming in, and I didn't know what I was going to do, but I put my trust in God. Some brothers from the church came out and cut the grass that I had already contracted to do. That brought in a little money. Our pastor, Bishop Harris, was there for me, as I knew he would be. The church took up special offerings and came by to encourage us.

Then the neighborhood got together and sent in checks and solicited funds, opening a bank account to receive them. Holy Trinity and other churches gave us financial support. We didn't miss a meal, and the bills were paid. It was such a blessing to see how God took care of us. It also let us see that our involvement in the community was not a one-way relationship. We had given to the neighborhood in ways that they needed, and now they were giving to us to meet our needs. That's what "community" is all about.

During that time of convalescence, I learned to appreciate my wife as never before. I could not do anything. I couldn't even brush my teeth, wash my ears, or even give myself a shower or bath. My wife had to do all that for me. I was a helpless invalid, but Mary was there in all her strength and love. Without mumbling or complaining, she cared for my every need and nursed me back to health.

Top left: Olgen's father, Mike Williams, born 1907 in Louisiana, died 1960 in Tennessee.

Top right: Olgen's mother, Jimmy Irene Webb, born 1925 in Tennessee, died 1993 in Indiana.

Bottom: Olgen graduated from Shortridge High School, Indianapolis, in 1966.

Top: Olgen Williams with U.S. Attorney General Janet Reno (center) and AFSCME union local 725 president Steven Quick (right), Indianapolis, 1999.

Middle: Olgen with Indianapolis Mayor Steve Goldsmith, 1999.

Bottom: Olgen Williams with U.S. Supreme Court Justice Clarence Thomas, Indianapolis, March 8, 2000.

Top: Olgen received the National Alumni of the Year Award from United Neighborhood Centers of America, Washington, D.C., September 2000.

Middle: Olgen Williams received his Master of Arts in Urban Ministry degree from President Boniface Hardin of Martin University, Indianapolis, January 2001.

Bottom: Since 1994, Near Westside residents of Indianapolis have organized annual community unity marches against drugs and violence.

Top: Olgen in his office at Christamore House, discussing his latest Westside project. The walls of his office are covered with his numerous awards for community service. July 2001.

Middle: Olgen Williams stands at the doorway of Christamore House, Indianapolis, April 2001.

Bottom: The Williams family at home, Indianapolis, September 2001. Back row: Aaron, David, Nicole, Jonathan. Middle row: Olgen Michael, Olgen Sr., Mary, Tim, Jason. Front row: Joi.

The Church & the City

At my church, I had been ordained as an elder, and God had blessed and used me there during the years Mary and I had been together. When my best friend, Elder William L. Harris Sr., and his wife, Sister Linda R. Harris, felt God calling them to start a new church, I felt God wanted me to go to help him. Mary and I prayed, and God gave us assurance that we were supposed to join the Harrises in their work.

We started the church in the apartment of Brother Robert Hall and his wife. There were about nine of us meeting just for Bible classes. The Lord really started blessing us, and, after a few weeks, we moved our meetings to Elder Paul Otis's church building, where I began to teach Sunday school and help out in worship. After we were there several months, God helped us to find a building to rent on our own at 16th and Alabama, right next door to a gay bar. The building was old and really a mess. We went in there and painted and made repairs and bought chairs. We fixed up the restroom. The office was in the basement— wet, musty, and full of spider webs—but we cleaned and worked on it. We were proud of our little space, and we sat there in that little building on the

73

and praised God and gave Him glory and thanks for
e had done for us and how He had blessed us.

People began to come in. They came in right off the
streets. Some were full of alcohol and had all kinds of problems
as they came stumbling in, but they would come in and sit in
the services. Sometimes those going to the white gay bar next
door would stumble into the wrong door by mistake and find
themselves surrounded by a bunch of Pentecostals with their
hands raised, saying, "Hallelujah to Jesus," and having a good
time in the Spirit. Of course, they were puzzled and shocked,
but some of them would stay. Several of them were eventually
baptized as they came and prayed and gave their lives to God.

We learned a lot about human beings down there and
about humility as well. People who came in off the streets full
of alcohol often hadn't bathed in months or even years. But
the pastor used to tell us that no matter how they came in, we
had to show them love. He emphasized that we had to endure
that smell and the annoying situation because those people
were watching us to see how we would react, and we needed
to show them God's love. We learned to put our arms around
them, to share what we had with them, and to let them know
that Jesus Christ did love them. Their lives could be better
because somebody cared about them. It was a rich experience
for us there. Victory has been a blessed church, and we are
now in our third place of worship, a building God enabled us
to purchase.

From about the second year after accepting Christ, I
had begun teaching Sunday school, and I had been studying
the Bible, taking all sorts of classes, building an extensive li-

brary of religious materials and literature, and sharing God's Word in various ways. Therefore, when the church grew to the point of needing a Sunday school superintendent, Elder Harris appointed me to that position. We now have about 95% of our Victory Tabernacle Church members coming to Sunday school every week. (They may come late, but they do come.) In addition to serving our local church, I was also blessed to be elected the state superintendent of the Sunday school for the district that includes Illinois, Indiana, and Wisconsin, and to bring together the teachers from the thirteen churches in that council twice a year for classes.

God gives each of us both spiritual and natural gifts and gives us ministries in which to use those gifts. He has given me the gifts of "helps" and administration and has opened up a lot of opportunities for me to serve Him—including helping with our church administration; serving as treasurer and accountant; preaching at times; teaching and counseling; working with young people; performing weddings and funerals; and conducting seminars and speaking before various audiences. When I think back to where I've come from, it makes me both humbled and grateful to see that God can use me.

I feel especially blessed when it comes to working with the people of the street, with their substance abuse and the multitude of other problems that come with that lifestyle. Being a former dopehead, I can empathize with them and share with them the things of Christ that I've learned. Whether I am dealing one-on-one with an alcoholic on the street or speaking before a national organization, I'm just thankful for what God has done in my life and very much aware that everything I know and everything I have to offer others is from God.

Even as a child, I wanted my life to have a purpose; like my unique name, I wanted to fulfill a unique place in this world. After becoming a Christian, I felt even more strongly that God had created me for a reason and that He had something He wanted to accomplish with my life. I had all this knowledge, this desire to help others, this zeal for service, and it seemed there just wasn't enough outlet for it. Even with my work in the church and my work with Maranatha, I still felt that somewhere there was a broader outlet for service.

Just before Marathon closed, I started getting involved in my own neighborhood, in my own community. This came about after Christina Lewis, a senior citizen active in the neighborhood organization, came down to the local barbershop one day and asked us young men if we would help out the Haughville Community Council and get involved in the Westside Cooperative Organization (WESCO). She explained that the seniors were the ones who had been carrying it for years, but they were getting old and needed someone to come and to take their place and help them accomplish more. Little did she know that her simple request would start my life on an entirely new road and eventually bring about a major change in our neighborhood.

The brothers and I had sat down at that barbershop day after day for years, solving all the world's problems. For over twenty years, I had been praying for the world and talking about the love of Christ and what we need to do, but I hadn't really done a whole lot. I always had a desire to help people and to be more than what people perhaps thought I would be. I'm by no means the most intelligent person in the world, but I have learned to use what God has given me. Now, because God had taken so many years to mold and shape me, I was almost ready; in fact, I was ready to be used by Him in greater service. I stepped out, ready to get involved in the community.

At that time, in 1993, the city had a new mayor. Here in the Haughville neighborhood, we had some big problems. An incident had occurred in which drug dealers shot two fire marshals who had been investigating some arson activity, paralyzing one of the marshals. The city was panicking. Haughville had a bad reputation for being a tough place full of dope sellers; 10th and Pershing was a place where there were plenty of drugs and drinking all the time and lots of people hanging out. The 900-block of Concord was a place where crack was available twenty-four hours a day, seven days a week.

The U.S. Attorney's Office for Indiana, along with Attorney General Debra Daniels, decided to see if the city would be interested in a program called Weed and Seed, sponsored by the Department of Justice, that involves two important strategies: law enforcement and community policing (weeding); and neighborhood restoration and prevention, intervention, and treatment (seeding). They presented the program to the near-Westside residents to see if we wanted to apply for a grant designation as a Weed and Seed city. The neighborhood started convening meetings, with thirty to forty people at each session—wheelers and dealers, big shots, police chief, deputy chief, Urban League president, judges, doctors, lawyers; it seemed as if most everybody was at these meetings. I went to my first meeting down at Goodwill Industries. I sat in a room and listened to what was going on, but I didn't know nothing from nothing about what they were talking about. All I knew is that they were going to start pulling in abandoned cars; that was one of their strategies because that seemed to be causing a problem in the neighborhood.

The next meeting was held at Christamore House, and further meetings were conducted a couple times a month. During this process, the city received some money from the Annie E. Casey Foundation to do some neighborhood assessment and planning. Because of the incident with the fire marshals and the unrest that caused, the city decided to use the money on the Westside area.

The initial strategy sounded simple enough: get the people together, get the neighbors involved, and let them begin to plan for a safer neighborhood. It sounded simple, but it's harder to do than it sounds. It is hard to get neighborhood people together who have been living in apathy and who have a mistrust of city government and the police department. The one thing the Weed and Seed program did for us was to bring us together in an organizational structure that allowed us to plan the total vision to reshape our neighborhood.

At one of the meetings, the question came up about how to inform the neighborhood, and a town meeting was suggested. Even though some people were opposed to the idea, I thought it was a good one, so I raised my hand and spoke out in favor of it. Another young man, Paul Ingram, also raised his hand and supported the idea. That little act of raising our hands and saying we thought the idea was a good one for our neighborhood got the two of us appointed to a committee to take the lead in organizing the town meeting. Mayor Steve Goldsmith and Deputy Mayor Nancy Silvers Rogers both attended. We had an auditorium full of people, and we had a good dialogue between the neighborhood and the city officials. That was the first time I had facilitated a neighborhood meeting, and I felt blessed of the Lord that it went well.

The consensus from the neighborhood was that we should proceed, so a core group was formed, and I was named co-chair. It was our responsibility to plan the Weed and Seed strategy. Key government people served as part of the core group, but they wanted the neighborhood to take the lead and to facilitate the process. After some serious planning and strategizing, we submitted a proposal to the Department of Justice, and eventually the area was designated a Weed and Seed site. This initial designation had no money attached, but it did mean we could be considered for funds in the future.

One of the major benefits of this process is that it brought together the three connecting but diverse neighborhoods of Haughville, Stringtown, and Hawthorne to work together to evaluate the situation and identify our common problems. Stringtown is a neighborhood of about 75% Caucasians, primarily Appalachian whites. Hawthorne is about 80% white, blue-collar workers. Haughville is about 70% African American. The black and white neighborhoods have traditionally been divided by an invisible barrier somewhere around Michigan Street.

Since kids from the three neighborhoods went to Washington High School together, there was some degree of relationship, but they still used to throw rocks at each other and experience other racial problems. Neighborhood feuding wasn't anything new. Even earlier, when Haughville was all white, the two sides opposite Michigan Street didn't get along, because one side was made up of Irish and German Catholics, while the other side was populated by Slovenian Catholics; they were separated by their language and ethnic differences. That's why Holy Trinity was built less than a mile from St. Anthony's, another big Catholic church. Over the years since World War II, the neighborhoods changed racially, especially Haughville. That's when the issues centered more on race than ethnicity.

One of the things we tried to do, however, in the Weed and Seed strategy was to let the whole neighborhood know that it is for everyone's benefit. Being a co-chair and eventually steering committee president, I had to work on how to pull together a diverse neighborhood like that. Coming from the late '60s and being radical and racist myself, I understood how deeply ingrained those feelings were, but I knew how Jesus had changed my thinking and taught me to love all of my brothers and appreciate all mankind. It took much praying, but with God's help, we were able to continue with the strategy.

Working Together to Make a Difference

At the end of 1993, I was approached about becoming president of the WESCO. I told those who asked me that I would accept only if no one else wanted the job. Since WESCO represents three diverse neighborhoods, I didn't want a divisive election that would start my tenure with bad feelings from the other two neighborhoods. In previous years, there had been some problems because one of the neighborhoods felt misrepresented by the leadership. As it turned out, mine was the only name on the ballot, and I was elected unanimously. The election as a whole worked out well, with all three neighborhoods represented in various leadership roles.

WESCO started me on the path of community leadership development. The others and I learned by doing. We had to keep Weed and Seed alive, so we strategized together, dealing with code compliance and environmental issues. In doing so, we became more organized and efficient. We began to have meetings with representatives from the police department and started to forge better neighborhood–police relationships. We needed additional funding to work on other projects, so we decided to apply for another grant.

We got together a team of ten people who wrote the proposal. Nobody thought we would receive the funding, and we were even laughed at for trying. To be honest, we were as shocked as anyone when we received $629,000. This was the first time our community had received a grant of this magnitude to plan a strategy. We were ecstatic. When we got the money, we hired Tyrone Chandler to direct the initiative. He was a young man who had worked in the Boy Scout's executive office and was living in the United Northwest Association (UNWA) neighborhood. He had graduated from our local Washington High School and from Purdue University.

It was while working with WESCO that I fell off the ladder and became injured. Eventually, I got my cast removed and was ready to return to work. At the same time, I was offered a job through Weed and Seed in a program called Hammerwest. My business had suffered during my absence, and we lost a major contract, so I decided just to close it down and take this new offer. This job was working with first-time drug offenders who were on probation or under house arrest. My work was to counsel, mentor, and supervise them as they worked on some small construction jobs and received a little stipend for their work.

This was a rewarding job for me, and I had good rapport with the young men because I understood them, having come from the streets myself. We respected one another. One of the young men was able to get off house arrest because of the changes that occurred in him as a result of our mentoring.

The youngest guy, just sixteen years old, came from the Hawthorne neighborhood. He had dropped out of school and had no self-motivation. I began counseling with him about drugs and the dead end of street life. His mother noticed big changes in him and told him that working with us was the best thing that ever happened to him.

During this same time, I had been serving on the board of the Christamore House, a "Christian Settlement House in Indianapolis on the order of Hull House in Chicago," as it was described at the time of its establishment in 1905. After two directors left that position in a short period of time, I was asked to serve as interim director. Rev. Julius Jackson was especially supportive of my playing that role, because one of the things I kept stressing as a board member was the need to get the community more involved. At that time, there weren't too many activities going on at Christamore House; it wasn't well connected with the community, and the neighborhood was disappointed in it. I took a leave of absence from the Hammerwest job and came to Christamore on February 28, 1996, to run a community service center with fourteen employees and a budget of over $300,000.

When it came time to hire a permanent director, I told them during my interview what I sincerely believed to be the truth—that they might find somebody who seemed more qualified than I in terms of degrees and professional experience, but that I didn't think anyone would love this place or have as much zeal for the work as I have. In April of 1996, I was hired permanently to run the center. It has been a very good experience for me, and I feel that our center is second to none in activities and growth. I love my work and look forward to Monday mornings. It amazes me that God gave me the opportunity to support my family by doing something I love.

As part of the Weed and Seed strategy we worked to make our neighborhood safer. We wanted to reduce drugs and alcoholism. In a major effort, we targeted a liquor store at 10th and Pershing where a lot was happening on the premises. Drug sales were going on, a murder had taken place on the lot, prostitution and drinking were common outside the building.

Several of us, including the president of Haughville Community Council, Jimmie Harrington Jr., began to fight to close it down for the sake of our community. Not only was the place a public nuisance but it also perpetuated crime and safety problems. We took time to gather photos and other evidence and eventually took the owners to court. It took a couple of years, but finally, on the last day of the year in 1996, that store was closed. We learned that by working together, strategizing, and being persistent in our efforts, we could effect positive change in our neighborhood.

It had been on the Weed and Seed project that I first began working with Deputy Mayor Nancy Silvers Rogers. It was easy to develop that relationship because her constant theme was "We want to help you; we want you to tell us how we can do that; we want you at the head of the table." Like most people, I love being in charge of my own destiny.

Mayor Stephen Goldsmith was an out-of-the-box Republican. Sincere in his desires, his major goal wasn't to please his party but instead to build a healthy city. He often worked contrary to the political structure; in fact, he shifted the Republican Party's philosophical paradigm on how to help neighborhoods. He initiated "compassionate conservatism" long before others ever thought of the concept. He was frugal in his use of money and held accountable those organizations to which money was given, but he was willing to step back and allow neighborhoods to control their own destiny. He made available to the public the funds that the public had entrusted to his keeping, allowing us to use those resources to better our communities. He was willing to help those willing to help themselves.

The Spring 1999 issue of *Blueprint* published an article I wrote, entitled "Caring for Our Civic Souls: Indianapolis' Front Porch Alliance." The article highlighted the importance of city government working together with community-based organizations to improve the neighborhoods and outlined some of the ways Mayor Goldsmith's Front Porch Alliance initiative did just that. In *Blueprint,* I wrote:

> The Front Porch Alliance doesn't run programs. . . .
> The Front Porch Alliance is a partnership between
> City Hall and the values-shaping institutions of Indianapolis. It coordinates civic groups and government agencies to empower local communities to
> run their own programs to improve Indianapolis'
> neighborhoods. . . . Working from the principle that
> government must first do no harm to the institutions of civil society, it enables them to expand the
> good work they already do.

Having lived in Indianapolis for forty-one years, I have witnessed firsthand the suffering inflicted on our weakest citizens by several decades of crime, drug use, fleeing businesses, poor health services, and broken homes. I have also seen neighborhoods rise up from this destruction, and I know what is required to revitalize them.

Government-only "solutions," no matter how well intentioned, are not enough to empower people. Real solutions are found when common people work together to create results. In order to bring health to our communities, there must be cooperation among government agencies, churches, synagogues, mosques, neighborhood organizations, schools, labor unions, charities, businesses, and citizens.

Neighborhood organizations, religious groups, and local businesses—together with government—are able to leverage substantial change in their communities. The trouble is that these groups are often disconnected from each other, unaware of how much more they could achieve by working together.

Instead of connecting these local institutions to each other and to the resources they need, government often blocks progress in neighborhoods by bringing in its own solutions without listening to the people on the ground. This doesn't mean that government should throw up its hands and walk away, leaving the problems in someone else's lap. Government can play a positive role by helping community-based groups form the partnerships they need to succeed in the work they are doing. That is the simple but strong conviction at the heart of Indianapolis's Front Porch Alliance.

When the City and the neighborhood leaders of WESCO began to work together to write a strategy to be designated as a federal Weed and Seed site, Mayor Goldsmith brought in Robert Woodson from the National Center for Neighborhood Enterprise (NCNE) to work with us. The NCNE has an academy at their headquarters in Washington, D.C., where they would take neighborhood people for a series of quarterly sessions to become community leaders. For this project, however, they decided to bring the training on site. Bob Woodson and Willamina Bell Taylor came to Indianapolis and sat down with city officials. They chose seven target neighborhoods, and those of us who were invited to participate attended workshops and seminars in the Beech Grove area of town. The NCNE began training us in areas of leadership and development.

One of our interesting assignments was to figure out what we would do if we were given $50,000 to use in our neighborhoods. After that, the city actually gave us some real money that we used to hire a neighborhood coordinator. We sat down and had a neighborhood planning strategy and wrote a job description for the new neighborhood coordinator, someone who could help me and the rest of us who were volunteer leaders. We hired Karen O'Connor, who fit the description of what we needed, and we ended up with one of the best neighborhood coordinators in the city.

Bob Woodson taught us about neighborhood empowerment and how to work with city officials to accomplish our goals. We took that message to heart and began to push for empowerment of our neighborhood. Before long, city officials left the table and began to sit in the audience, while we decided what was best for our own neighborhood.

There was one memorable lapse in the city's determination to acknowledge us as full partners. Without telling us they had even applied, the city got a $3,500,000 Youth Fair Chance grant, targeting the WESCO and UNWA neighborhoods. Of course, this was a wonderful thing, allowing us to make systematic changes in the neighborhood to benefit young people from fourteen to thirty years old, but it put us in an awkward position when we weren't informed that it was even on the drawing board. One day I was asked to attend a meeting at Goodwill regarding neighborhood issues. When I got there, there were media representatives, TV cameras, and an air of excitement. Even when I asked what was going on, I was told nothing until the public announcement was made about the receipt of the grant; then I was asked at that same moment to go to the mike and say something. Being totally ignorant of what it was all about, I tried to ad lib something appropriate in front of the cameras, but it was an awkward moment. It's at those times, though, that you have to set aside your own feelings and think about the good of the neighborhood. This grant was a wonderful opportunity to help our youth. School-to-work programs and youth job programs were started with this money, and the results are still with us today. Projects with the city have continued. For instance, the city bought land from a church, helped clean it up, and then helped to establish a three-million-dollar health clinic on the site.

Community Development Block Grants were another source of funding that helped us. Each neighborhood was given a grant to use as it saw fit. Some neighborhoods used it to fix up houses or make property improvements, but we used the money to build service capacity. We started several initiatives aimed at children and youth: an after-school program (offering a safe haven, tutoring, mentoring and other activities); a computer program; a summer program; and a character development program (teaching social skills, taking the kids on field trips, and building their potential). We wanted to invest in kids, not in brick and mortar.

A Hope VI grant from HUD put about thirty million dollars into renovating Concord Village, a public housing community in the neighborhood that was full of drug trafficking, violence, and shooting. Through this funding, the tenants were moved out, the structures were rebuilt, and in 1999 the residents were moved back into single-family homes. Social service programs have been initiated; there are nice yards and a well-lit parking area; it has become a place where people really want to live. The result has been that an area that once held the record for the highest crime rate in Indianapolis now has the lowest; there is less crime in this public housing community than anywhere else in the city.

We got other grants, including one from the Greater Indianapolis Progress Committee (GIPC) to start a newsletter and another grant to do an information brochure and mailings for our WESCO organization. As we as a neighborhood collaboration began to pull together, we started to see changes.

With crime as one of the major problems in the Westside community, we needed to learn to work with the police and to recognize a common goal: to make our streets safe and our community one we could be proud of—a neighborhood where the drug dealers would be the ones afraid to be on the streets, not the neighbors who lived there. Community policing was an issue that Mayor Goldsmith wanted to explore because the neighborhood had no trust of the police community. So we met with the police and began to strategize at neighborhood meetings on community policing. As we began to meet together, we started getting to know them and they got to know us. Deputy Chief Bob Allen was on board at that time; he was a good man, worked well with us, and was willing to help us.

There was a lot of negative history between the police and the residents on the Westside. In order for this new partnership to work, we had to be willing to forgive, to wipe the slate clean, to build trust, and to have faith that it would work. The police, on the other hand, had to be assured that as a neighborhood we were on the side of law and order, that we would back the police when they were doing their job. Working together, the police and the neighborhood opened the lines of communication and began to get issues into the open.

The concept of community policing began in full force when Deputy Chief Jerry Barker began to work on the Westside. He is a great guy, and he was willing to listen to our concerns and our insider's view about what needed to be done. Leading the way in this new effort, Deputy Chief Barker began eating his lunch in the 900-block of Concord just to show a police presence. Bike patrols began working the streets. The police came to community meetings. Officers became involved in youth activities—sponsoring a basketball tournament, hosting a bike repair shop, taking kids to Pacers games, and doing other things to show they cared. Residents began to feel safe and secure while criminals started feeling insecure.

We began to make inroads in community policing to the point that we have one of the finest policing communities in the city of Indianapolis, and perhaps the whole state. I went from knowing only one police officer out here (one who happened to go to the same barbershop) to knowing almost everyone from the deputy chief down to the rookies. We have been involved in the interviewing process used in hiring those people for our community.

We can call the police anytime, and they will come out and help us. This was a huge change. We honored the police for their work one day by having food available to feed them during their shifts and then had a ceremony where we gave plaques and other tokens of appreciation. The police later honored some of the community leaders at a special dinner. A real relationship was built between the police and the neighborhood. In the process, the crime rate went down. Haughville became the first neighborhood in Indianapolis to reduce the homicide rate by 70 percent (in 1997).

Community policing worked so well that other law enforcement agencies have come to ask us how they can become more involved in helping the community. In fact, we now have people from the FBI, U.S. Marshals, the U.S. Attorney's Office, the Department of Tobacco and Firearms, and the Drug Enforcement Agency all participating with us. Some participate in meetings, others serve on boards, some are involved in programs with kids, and many take part in community activities.

Throughout the years of our work, we have continued to learn to collaborate with others. First, it was with each other; then with the mayor's office; then with the police department. Now we are involved in collaborations or partnerships with over sixty-five other agencies. One such relationship has been with Indiana University–Purdue University at Indianapolis (IUPUI). In a three-year program, the university has provided tutors and mentors for kids, help in preschool and camp programs, assistance for seniors in working on their houses, and help in beautifying the neighborhood by planting flowers and doing other such projects.

Another dramatic change we are proud of is the reduction of our infant mortality rate on the Westside. Working with the university and others, we began to address the issue; the infant mortality rate had once been at a high of 21 percent. Now the rates have dropped dramatically as a combined result of the following efforts:

- focusing on a holistic, healthy, caring environment;
- emphasizing education, especially of young women;
- opening a good health clinic; and
- building trust in agencies housed in the neighborhood. The latest figures show the infant mortality rate in Haughville at 3.5 percent.

It takes a concerted effort on the part of a lot of people to turn a neighborhood around. One such group of men, called Westside Concerned Dads, has served in a variety of ways, including

- mentoring kids;
- granting scholarships to youth;
- facilitating in-school workshops on topics such as conflict resolution and giving and getting respect; and
- walking the streets on weekends to serve as light, exposing and driving out the darkness. Another organization, the Westside Business Association, has gotten started; as a result of their work, twenty-seven new businesses have begun. In 1999, the Westside Community Development Corporation built thirty-nine houses and rehabbed eleven. One successful effort leads to another.

There are several lessons I've learned over the years about the grassroots approach to neighborhood improvement.

- It requires sacrificial leadership.
- Hundreds of people must be involved; nothing can be done alone.
- People must be willing to engage in forgiveness, trust-building, and faith.
- Focusing on issues of politics, race, and religion can distract from the main goals of the organization—things like getting chuck holes filled, closing crack houses, bringing in new business, etc.
- The emphasis must stay on the common things that bind us together, not the differences that separate us. For instance, we celebrate neighborhood success, not diversity. We celebrate growth in neighborhood business, not in growth of black or white businesses.
- It is crucial to have the support of the city admini-

stration. So much depends on the funding decisions and regulations set by the city that, outside of a relationship with those leaders, it would be nearly impossible to see much accomplished.

Everyone in a neighborhood is chiefly concerned about the same things. On the Westside, we have identified our key areas of concern: education, economic development, affordable housing, security and safety. Rather than trying to create new services to improve these areas, we have learned to build relationships and partner with others, using services already available within the larger community. Relationships are always evolving and rarely perfect. Even in our work with Mayor Goldsmith and with the police department, there were issues that arose, but we worked through them and developed wholesome and healthy relationships.

In November of 1999, the citizens of Indianapolis elected their first Democratic mayor in thirty-two years. Bart Peterson was the person elected. He ran against a good friend of mine, Sue Ann Gilroy. I supported her during the election, but I thought Bart would make a good mayor also.

In a pre-election meeting with Mayor Peterson, I informed him that if he got elected, I would support him to make Indianapolis a world-class city. We have a good relationship with the city staff because we have the same goals when it comes to making Indianapolis greater.

After Mayor Peterson started office, he picked some great people for his staff. Two people in particular I think were the best. The first is Public Safety Director Robert Turner, a former Indianapolis Police Department officer. Mr. Turner had been very active in the Indianapolis community for decades, and I always thought him to be very straightforward and outspoken.

The other person is former Deputy Chief of Police Jerry Baker. After interviewing several candidates for chief of police, the mayor chose Jerry. I had worked with Chief Baker for over seven years on the Westside. Because of his work with us, we created the best community-policing program in the city.

To be successful, a neighborhood has to have training, encouragement, leadership development, and resources. The leaders need to know how to kindle hope in the people, how to send forth a rallying cry and get people not just motivated but also activated. They need also to help the people create success and help them to understand it was through their efforts that something was accomplished. Leaders need to constantly be cheerleaders and let the people know they can do what they set their minds to do. After a few successes, this lesson will hit home, and people will begin to see it for themselves. Leaders need to get some things done quickly, to show themselves as agents of change in the neighborhoods. People flock to work with those who get things done.

My Philosophy of an Urban Church Ministry

Altruism is a basic Christian trait. The true Christian looks past race, social standing, financial status, family name, religious persuasions, and dress and just loves people!

Jesus said, "This is the first and great commandment. And the second is like unto it, Thou shalt love thy neighbour as thyself" (Matthew 22:38–39). Loving people is next to loving God. Jesus emphasized the importance of this principle by making it the second commandment, but He likened it to the first and great commandment. Further, He went on to say that all the law hangs on these two greatest commandments; that is to say, all the Old Testament develops and amplifies these two points.

The urban church ministry should influence the neighborhood. Its presence needs to be a blessing to the community. The urban church ministry can assist the community in resisting and regulating bars, liquor shores, pornography shops, and other undesirable elements. The ministry must stand as a moral leader in such matters.

People should come to know the church ministry for its positive influence in the community and also for its leadership in practical matters. Things such as keeping the neighborhood neat and clean may not be issues pertaining to salvation, but they are important in establishing the urban church ministry members as good citizens and neighbors.

The urban church ministry can also provide excellent community services, such as daycare for children, drug and alcohol abuse support, marriage counseling, safe-driving classes, youth activities, and other services. Perhaps the urban church ministry could make its facilities available free of charge for such community activities as town meetings, a shelter, and weddings. These activities will make a church vulnerable to many problems, but they also will contribute to a positive image of the church in the community. The urban church ministry will become a vital part of the community.

If one believes, as I do, in the worth of all of God's living human beings, and that our personal welfare as ministers and teachers of God is inextricably bound up with all of our brothers' and sisters', it follows that anyone's poverty of goods or spirit or pleasure impoverishes all; and that our contributions to God's work be of a quality to emphasize this respect for humankind, whether we choose to be a laborer, an artisan, a poet, a musician, a teacher, a physician or a social worker or preacher of the Gospel, or Sunday school superintendent.

Quality is dependent upon temperamental aptitude and knowledge. The former governs one's choice of work; the latter is a constantly growing collection of skills which we gather as we go along. The sources of knowledge are records of what has been done in the past; what we have learned in educational institutions; current experiments which we share with workers in the same and related fields; our personal daily experiments; and the knowledge that God has given to us.

From the wide area of church urban ministry work one chooses a specialty, as a musician chooses to play a violin, a doctor chooses to concentrate in pediatrics. But a specialist must know something of the whole wide field within which he/she has chosen. Then one decides in which framework to apply his/her trade: as an overseer over a flock, a teacher, as a resident in a children's institution, or a private practitioner. I have chosen to work in the urban community for its color, its diversity, and its possibilities for growing. This is my idea of an urban church community ministry and the workers who are called to social action.

An urban church ministry should be a ministry that serves the church and community. This means each minister (servant) or teacher must be glad of his/her work and secure in his/her calling from God in order to extend security and gladness to those whom they minister to. He/She must have the skills appropriate to his/her particular ministry, and have the basic skills in working with people, which sometimes is a fine balance between intellect and Holy Spirit guidance.

An urban church ministry should be active in the neighborhoods of the residents that it serves. While it may be in a community where there are limitations to living and playing, the ministry should provide leadership so that its residents may reach beyond the bounds of their physical and spiritual environment. To offer experience in the beauty of life and knowledge of God, and acquaintance with many kinds of people should be part of the plan. Learning is frequently painful for those who have been living in ignorance of their power to change. The ministry is a tool to provide leadership through the pain to the rewarding pleasures beyond it.

A ministry cannot be isolated in time and space, but must be consciously linked with the past and the future, and concerned with constructive social change. This means that the present always contains part of the good history; that in acknowledgment of what we have learned from our predecessors here, and in similar ministries elsewhere, we contribute our learning to the common pool, and help to train leaders for the future. It means that we keep ourselves aware of what is being done currently, and give our support to movements that will implement work carried on in a philosophy like ours.

An urban church ministry must be cooperative. Members should feel affectionate toward it. They should be able to use what it offers. Use of its services should always be a step toward strengthening their resources, so that they may become self-reliant contributors to the church community in their own right.

An urban church ministry should be dynamic. Its services should be developed to meet the needs it discovers through intimate fellowship with members of the church community. Its workers should have the courage to initiate new plans, and to discard outmoded programs. They should refrain from undertaking a job the ministry is ill equipped to do, but should exert effort and influence to see that such jobs are done by an appropriate ministry. When new services are

projected, careful planning should ensure the
the community, and the space and time
adequate to guarantee a reasonable hope .
need not be confined within the walls at a particu.
dress; rather, it should so extend that it permeates the .
borhood, and becomes part of the whole life of its residents.

In the face of overwhelming need everywhere, we maintain our equilibrium only through the exercise of patience and faith and love. The patience is for long-term planning. The faith is that everything we do may weigh in on the happiness side of the scale for our church community. Love is the bond of perfection that will hold it all together.

A Life Fulfilled

Because of my commitment to my church and to my neighborhood, my life will never be the same. Instead of rapping with the guys in the barbershop and accomplishing nothing, I have been invited to serve on various committees in the city; have been interviewed by television media; have been asked to give speeches to groups of federal executives in Washington, D.C.; have met with mayors; and have counseled with every type of law enforcement agency in the state as well as the FBI—all of which helped to make a genuine difference. If I had stayed in the barbershop, my life might have been simpler and easier, but I would never have known the feeling I have now—that my life is really making a difference, that I am actually able to make good things happen for the people I care about.

I am a fortunate man in being able to do these things, but I never forget that it isn't because of my own natural intelligence and ability; it's by the grace of God that I'm able to participate. It isn't the Olgen Williams who was born on September 14, 1948, whom you see as a leader in the Westside

103

community, but the Olgen Williams who was born again on April 28, 1972. The former Olgen Williams would have been part of the problem, not part of the solution; he would have been one of the guys hanging out at the liquor store, drinking and doing drugs, not one of the men closing it down.

Before I turned my life over to Christ, I would not have been invited to sit at the table with community leaders; in fact, I didn't even like those people.

But God changed me and put within my heart a desire to do the right thing for the good of all people. He took out of my heart the racism, the rebellion against authority, the self-centered lifestyle, and the need to feel important; instead, He put within me a real love for all people, the willingness to serve others, a genuine concern for other people, and the security of knowing I'm important to God, so it doesn't matter so much what others think about me.

God changed me, but He didn't make me perfect. I still struggle with things, and I still have to depend on God every day to keep me on track and to work in my character the qualities that He wants. But I'm blessed by all that He has done already and I trust Him to continue to work in and through my life.

Christamore House is a unique place. Our goal is to put people on the road to self-sufficiency; my mission is to help people help themselves. God has blessed us since I've been here, and we have seen a rapid growth of programs, activities, and funding, and we have seen big changes in people's lives. In this job, I am able to do counseling not only with my staff but also with neighborhood people, the homeless, youth, and those challenged by domestic violence or other problems. I can see how God prepared me for this job, first by changing me from the inside out and then by giving me experience in counseling and helping people in my church, at Hammerwest, and in the larger community. I don't take this opportunity to counsel others lightly. A verse in James says that if any man lack wisdom, he should ask of God. I am continually asking God for the wisdom and the knowledge to help other people. I don't want to just go through the motions, but I want to have the right words to say so that they will get some sense of direction and comfort and can go on to live their own lives in a way that will be rewarding for them.

Working at Christamore House has also been a blessing to our family. It has given me the chance to spend more time with my family, because they are involved in the things I do. The boys come and play basketball, work in our bicycle action project, and participate in other programs. I'm here working, but they're also here enjoying themselves. We have fellowship and connection; it's been a really great blessing for me to be able to work with the kids on a day-to-day basis. And not only our kids, but all of the neighborhood kids. All of this has been very rewarding.

A fulfilling life, however, doesn't mean an easy life, and doing the right thing doesn't always make you popular. Just to illustrate, I remember one Saturday morning while I was busy working at Christamore House when my pager began vibrating. My wife was paging me with a "911" message, informing me there was an emergency at home. When I called, she told me one of our next-door neighbors was yelling curses at her from their porch and threatening my life, saying that I was going to come up missing if I did not leave her alone. I ran to my van and drove straight home, only a few blocks away.

When I arrived, the woman was in her front yard in a rage. When she saw me, all of her anger and wrath was then vented in my direction. I walked to my front porch to check on Mary and my daughter and found that they were shaken but all right. I stood in my yard and could hear the man of that house talking to the woman; then he walked off the porch, asking her if she wanted him to shoot me now. I began walking back toward my van to move away from my family, and the man walked up to the fence to talk to me. I asked him bluntly if he was going to shoot me. If that was the case, I knew I couldn't stop him, so I just put my life in the hands of Jesus. He said he was not threatening me but just wanted to talk about the situation.

The woman was still raging in her front yard and began to talk even louder. She told me that I should mind my own business and leave her alone; a narcotics officer had informed her that I called the police about too much night traffic at her house, and now she was going to have to move out. The man and I started to talk about the situation. I quickly realized that he was high on something and that it would be hard to communicate with him.

I told him that I did not know his friend's name but that I was not going to allow her to disrespect my wife or family. I told him that I might take the verbal abuse, but I would not allow my wife to be disrespected. Surprisingly, he began to cry and agree with me. He said his friend was wrong for cursing around my children and that selling drugs should not be allowed in the community. We shook hands and embraced after a few minutes of conversation.

The incident, however, left me feeling unnerved. I could not believe that a police officer would give out that kind of information. The woman had been right. I had talked to the police about the traffic and my belief that crack cocaine was being sold out of the house. My suspicions had started several weeks before that Saturday. My dog, Max, started to bark every night around midnight. When I went to look out my kitchen window to see why he was barking, I noticed people moving through my neighbor's backyard. I watched this for about a week. Then people began knocking on my door past midnight, looking for my neighbor's house. After I saw a person I knew to be a drug user going into the house, I knew my suspicions were correct.

Shortly after that, I saw Deputy Chief Jerry Barker at a public event and told him about the situation on my street. Two days later, undercover police officers made an arrest and found crack in my neighbor's house and garage area. The police arrested a young man for selling drugs out of the house; he already had four outstanding warrants. My neighbor was not arrested, because she told the police the person arrested had made her let him use the house to sell drugs.

After that Saturday morning incident, I didn't know what to do. I began to have some fears about the safety of my wife and our family. I wanted the problem to just go away quickly, but it didn't. The next Sunday morning, when we went out to get in our van to go to church, we found that one of the windows had been broken out. I spoke with a friend in the Community Policing Program, and several police officers who heard about the situation wanted to come by my house to watch out for us or help out in some way. Not wanting to make the situation bigger, though, I declined their offer.

After talking together about what we should do, my wife and I decided the best way to deal with our problem was not to fight back but to pray to God. I knew I needed prayer, because I was more afraid of myself and what I might do than of the people next door. Before I became a Christian, I would not have considered turning the other cheek, and I did not want to revert to my old ways. My neighbor was fortunate that I cared about maintaining my Christian testimony; my inner desire to please God was a good thing for both my neighbor and me.

That Sunday, I asked the church to pray for my family, my neighbor, and me. God answered that prayer quickly. That very night, my neighbor moved out of the house, taking some of the owner's appliances with her on her way out. Eventually the house was sold, and our street, thanks to God and the police, remained free of drugs.

Just as God had prepared me for the work I do now at Christamore House, I believe He is continuing to prepare me for other experiences I'll have later on. Wanting to be ready for whatever He brings my way, I am continually looking for ways to improve myself and increase my effectiveness in working with others. One step I took that was a . was for me to go back to school. I had never really cε about getting a degree, and I felt I was too old and didnι time. But my board of directors was supportive, and the ι nances were provided, so I felt it was time to take another step forward. Also by setting this goal and furthering my own education, I thought I could set an example for my children, to encourage them to seek higher education.

I chose Martin University because of its urban learning environment and its Prior Learning Assessment (PLA) program. Dr. Thomas Brown came to the Christamore House's Board of Directors meeting and explained Martin University's Prior Learning Assessment program, which is a process to document, to evaluate, and to grant credit for a person's life experiences and out-of-classroom learning. The Board was willing to support me in my desire to complete college. I signed up for the PLA program under Dr. Skif Peterson, who was very encouraging to me and pushed me to complete my goal. He brought in former classmates to talk with us and to share the wonderful success of the program over the years.

Because of the semester I spent with Dr. Skif Peterson and his encouragement and his guidance in how to write an autobiography and to put together a portfolio documenting my life experience, I was successful. I was able to earn credit hours equivalent to over two years of college study, which encouraged me to go on with my schooling. You are witnessing his encouragement as you read these words, since my autobiography from PLA is the foundation for the book that you are reading.

After the semester break in 1996, I skipped the summer and then started classes in the fall. I started full-time in Martin University's Religious Studies Program. I took full-time courses from the time I started until I graduated in 1999.

I remember well the time and I signed up for my first English course, EN 125. I took my first pretest and did not do too well. The instructor told me, "You are a little rough on the edges, but you still could probably pass the course and get a good grade with a lot of hard work." So, I went to my mentor and asked to be put into English 096, which is basic English.

Dean Bobbie Jean Craig was my English instructor. She was straightforward, ran a tight ship; she was there to ensure that we learned our work. She tolerated no foolishness and led me to another level in preparing me for college. I was able to achieve academically in that class, and I became optimistic as I received an A–.

From that point on, I think that I received nothing less than an A– at Martin during my undergraduate work. I am really proud of that! I graduated summa cum laude and was awarded the President's Award at my graduation in 1999.

I then decided to pursue a Master of Arts Degree in Urban Ministry, focusing on the social action track. I was full speed ahead of the Master's Program, starting full-time in the summer of 1999 and graduating in January of 2001. I'm very proud of my academic accomplishments and of graduating with the President's Award.

Martin has a special place in my heart. I think it is one of the greatest institutions in our state. The instructors and staff are wonderful to work with. The time that they give you, the personal telephone numbers, and being able to call them whenever needed has been very heartening to me. I've never had a problem with any faculty or staff. The faculty have been willing to go the extra mile to help you achieve your best and to make sure that you learned.

I must take some space just to say a few words about two of the finest people I have come into contact with. They are Father Boniface Hardin, the President and Founder of Martin University, and Sister Jane Schilling, the Academic Vice President of Martin University. These two persons have been role models to me. Their dedication and sacrifices to the Martin community are second to none. I received nothing but encouragement from both of them. To be able to see our president walk down the hallways and enter our class to speak to us was great, and to have our vice president stop and talk with me and give me a hug or kiss was overwhelming at times. These acts of love and kindness are not found at the university level of education in most places.

As you read this book, I am planning to go back to school to obtain a doctoral degree. I am still part of Martin University, part of the Alumni Association. I try to stay connected and to do whatever I can to help my fellow university alumni stay successful and to assist in recruiting some of the finest students in the Indianapolis community.

I will always be grateful for the support of the Christamore Guild, my friends, my church, my family, my wife, and my savior, Jesus Christ. Martin has given me the educational skills that made me the person that I am today. By God's grace and mercy and by Martin University, I am a better person today. "Thanks for a great job!"

When I look back over my life and compare what could have happened with what actually did happen, I can only thank God. Instead of spending my life hanging out on the streets, I'm sitting at the table with dignitaries in high places. Instead of being a troublemaker and causing problems in the community, I'm running a community center. Instead of making fun of churchgoers, I'm teaching and preaching and participating in national conferences of church leaders. Instead of sitting back and criticizing my children's school system and being a complaining parent, I'm serving on school committees and mentoring school children.

Instead of selling drugs, I operated a legitimate business and helped create a business association for neighborhood economic development. Instead of repetitive trips to prison, I'm working together with the police and have seen our neighborhood crime and murder rate decline substantially as a result of our efforts. Instead of a lonely, self-centered existence, I have a wonderful, loving family. Instead of being dead from alcohol, drug abuse, or the war in Vietnam, I'm very much alive and wanting to make every minute of my life count.

These things are all blessings from God, not anything I can take credit for. Without Him, I know where I'd be. I'm not especially talented, or intelligent, or charismatic, and I'm certainly not rich; but God has still found ways to use me. He can do that for anyone. I'm not proud of some of the things that happened in my life; some of them have been painful to remember and even more painful to share openly for everyone to learn about. But that's the only way others can see the difference God has made in my life and can understand what He can do with a life in spite of the way we may have messed it up. He first transformed me, and then He used me to help transform my neighborhood. That is the message I wanted to pass on when I decided to share this story of my life. God first works on changing us inside as individuals, and then He uses us outside with others to help change our world.

My desire as I think about the remainder of my life is to be a servant to people, to my neighborhood, and especially to Christ. I hope I have even more opportunities in the future to draw on my experiences at Christamore House and WESCO to show others how to empower urban neighborhoods so that they can grow and prosper and become a place that residents are proud and content to call home.

Several things that have helped me in my work in my home neighborhood are the following:

- having a spirit to collaborate with other groups;
- looking at assets in the neighborhood; and
- going beyond the brick-and-mortar infrastructure and seeing what resources we have in the community—especially human capital that can be recruited and developed.

We find that most neighborhoods have assets that they are unaware of. The number-one assets are the families themselves. They are the residents who are willing and have chosen to live in the neighborhood, investing in it financially by buying a home or by renting a home in the neighborhood. They also invest in making sure that their children receive a proper education.

The rewards I get from my work are not monetary, but just being able to see people help themselves is my fulfillment. In many ways, though, I am a rich man. I have a good God, a great family, wonderful friends, and the privileged opportunity to make a difference in peoples' lives. I tell people there are three things that I love to talk about: the story of how God has changed my life; my wonderful wife and children; and a job that is a labor of love. And this is probably all I have to say about Olgen Williams. As the song says, "If anybody would ever write my life story, I would want him to just say that God has been good to me."

Westside Community Programs

The following pages list many of the community programs and services that Westside Cooperative Organization (WESCO) has developed, provided, and/or sponsored since 1996. If you or your group have proposals for other community-based programs or are interested in any of the programs on this list—as participant, volunteer, leader, organizer, fund-raiser, sponsor, donor—contact Christamore House.

Programs for Youth

Breakfast with the Boyz & Girlz

Empowers adolescent males and females in the areas of leadership, conflict resolution, and health issues through presentations and role-playing. Topics discussed are health, hygiene, leadership, and conflict.

Partners: Christamore House; Urban League (GITIT); Indianapolis Housing Agency; Westside Community Ministries, Inc. (WCMI)

Conflict Workshop

Shows youth an alternative healthy way to resolve conflicts and disputes without fighting.

Partners: Americorps

Indianapolis Inner City Youth Racing League (Soap Box Derby)

Children ages 9 to 16 work directly with an adult to create their own soap box derby cars. The experience teaches them craftsmanship, problem solving, and teamwork. The children are able to express their creativity, build confidence, and strengthen or form a relationship with an adult.

Partners: Indianapolis Motor Speedway, Indianapolis Weed & Seed,

Head and Neck Cancer Rehabilitation Institute, City of Indianapolis, Indy Parks, and local business community

Safe Haven

An after-school program for 6- to 18-year-olds, from 3 to 9 P.M., Monday through Friday. Provides tutoring, mentoring, sports, and recreational activities in a safe and supervised environment.

Partners: Weed & Seed/WESCO; Atkins Boys & Girls Club; Christamore House; Hawthorne Community Center; Stringtown; Lifeline Community Center; Indianapolis Police Department (IPD) West District; First Baptist North Family Courage Center

Survival Skills for Youth

A ten-session workshop that teaches life-skills to young men and women. Topics cover respect for self and others, legal rights and responsibilities, succeeding at work and school, and health.

Partners: Christamore House

Urban Explorers

This program offers participants social and recreational events, leadership skills training, community service opportunities, career education programs, and a wide variety of leadership opportunities.

Partners: Boy Scouts; Christamore House

WESCO Youth Council

Provides a platform for young people within the community to voice their opinions. Members of the Youth Council come

from the neighborhoods of Haughville, Hawthorne, Stringtown, Concord and Eagle Creek Village.
Partners: Christamore House; Hawthorne Community Center; Stringtown; Indianapolis Public Housing

Young Men on The Rise

A young men's group designed to teach responsibility as it relates to sexuality (including sexually transmitted diseases and adolescent pregnancies), social skills, and leadership skills. These important subjects are explored through information sessions, interactive group discussions, athletics, and field trips.
Partners: Healthy Start; School 90

Youth Living Responsibly

Monthly mentoring programs at area schools provide informative sessions on anger control, respect, and conflict resolution.
Partners: Westside Concerned Dads (WESCO DADS); Westside Community Ministries, Inc. (WCMI)

Programs for Women

Far From Home House

The first of its kind, this is a 100-year-old house that was turned into a two-year transitional housing program to assist homeless female veterans. six to eight women participate as occupants and contribute funding for their board on an individual need basis.

Partners: Hammerwest; Veterans Administration (VA); Disabled Veterans Administration (DAV); Far From Home Program; City of Indianapolis; State of Indiana; Federal Government

Sister for Sister

Designed to help girls to become aware of their options and to make effective and positive life decisions. Sister for Sister recognizes the control that girls have over events in their lives and presents life issues to girls as questions to be addressed based on their values, rather than as insurmountable problems that cannot be solved.

Partners: Christamore House; Big Sisters; Americorps

Survival Skills for Women

This program provides training, support, encouragement, and empowerment to move participants from powerlessness and low self-esteem toward personal well-being, confidence, and financial independence.

Partners: Christamore House

Welcome to Our Community

A program that targets first-time and other mothers in the Haughville area. The purpose of the group is the reduction of infant mortality. Participants meet monthly for dinner and a presentation. First-time participants receive a baby kit, and all members are offered babysitting, transportation, and gifts. Program components include Safe Sitter training, individual case management, and participant surveys.

Partners: Christamore House; MOM Project

Programs for Men

Survival Skills for Men

A core curriculum that promotes the learning of functional skills and uses examples and activities that directly relate to realistic circumstances. The program adheres to the educational methodologies of modeling, behavioral rehearsal, reinforcement, shaping, cognitive self-management, and generalization. It also builds on the strengths and experiences of the men in the group and cultivates support among participants.

Partners: Christamore House; Hammerwest; Community Residents; Community Churches; Marion County Jail Chaplaincy

Westside Concerned Dads (WESCO DADS)

Provides adult men representation in existing community-based programs. The WESCO DADS are community-concerned fathers and men banding together to accomplish common goals such as protection, development, and promotion of our youth.

Partners: Haughville Fathers

Programs for Families

Family Night

Designed to bring the families in the WESCO Community together for food, fun, prizes, and games to let residents know their neighbors, and to care about their neighborhood.

Partners: Christamore House; Hawthorne Community Center; Indianapolis Public Housing

Keeping Families Together

Helps to break the cycle of loneliness and alienation by bringing together loved ones who have been separated by prison bars. Enables close communication between the inmate and the family to maintain the much-needed sense of family. Gives inmates a reason to serve their time productively, with the expectation of being reunited with their families.

Parents Club

A support group for parents that meets monthly for dinner and speaker/discussion. Babysitting and transportation provided.

Partners: MOM Project; Christamore House

Community Programs

IPD Appreciation Day

Formed to help build the morale of the West District Officers. The Community Policing Committee went beyond the federal funds that Weed & Seed provides to show the positive feelings of the community towards the IPD Officers of the West District.

Partners: Indianapolis Police Department (IPD) West District; Community Residents; Community Businesses; Community Centers

Kingdom Come Workshops & Seminars

The curriculum is titled "Kingian Nonviolence." Specifically focuses on the techniques and strategies used by Dr. Martin Luther King Jr. to effect social change.

Weed & Seed Training Site (Expansion)

Trains the other sites about the Weed & Seed process: how to set up steering committees and sub-committees, how to work with Safe Havens, economic development, grant writing, and progress reports.

Partners: Westside Cooperative Organization (WESCO); United Westside Neighborhood Association (UNWA); Mid-North

Westside Community Ministries, Inc.

A partnership of Westside Cooperative Organization (WESCO), United Westside Neighborhood Association (UNWA), and other community organizations to unite and increase the capacity of Christian churches to strengthen families and enhance the quality of life for neighborhood residents of Westside Indianapolis and beyond.

Partners: Weed & Seed/WESCO, UNWA, Indianapolis Police Department (IPD) West District, Indiana Housing Agency; Christamore House; Juvenile Center Referrals; Local Churches

Education & Cultural Programs

ACT (Asante Children's Theatre)

A youth-based cultural arts organization that focuses upon education, enlightenment, and empowerment through the dramatic arts.

ACT Reading Celebration Club

This club assists children from pre-school to second grade develop their reading skills. All ACT players are required to volunteer at least 20 hours during the season to the community service project. The ACT performers read to and read with the younger children. They use their dramatic skills to act out stories to inspire the younger children to read.

Partners: Christamore House; Asante Children's Theatre

America Reads

Students are placed in various community centers and schools throughout Indianapolis to serve as reading tutors to children preschool through grade 6.

Partners: Indiana Literacy Foundation

Continued Learning After School Program (CLASP)

Activities include violin lessons, piano lessons, harmony choir, martial arts, boxing, basketball, tutoring, arts and culture, computer learning, community service projects, social development, open gym, and snacks.

Power Hour

A tutoring program to provide one-on-one tutoring in various subjects to improve youth educational opportunities.

Partners: Indiana University-Purdue University-Indianapolis (IUPUI) Work Study Students; Americorps

Job Training Programs

Bicycle Project

The project is designed to teach Weed & Seed youth the skills of bike repair and how to run a business. Youth are provided with tools to fix broken bikes and are taught the rules of the road.

Partners: Christamore House; Indianapolis Police Department (IPD) West District

Hammerwest

A 12-week hands-on, basic construction training and job preparation program. The program is funded by the Department of Justice though the Weed & Seed Initiative. The partners work together to help renovate housing in the neighborhoods while training and preparing the residents of Indy's Westside for well-paying jobs and career advancement. The curriculum covers general construction and carpentry in detail. Seminars on various life skills are offered as well as ongoing contact with the trainee's case manager. Although participants are students, not employees, they are expected to act as if they are on the job. Hammerwest pays eligible participants a stipend and provides needed tools during both classroom and field work. Eligibility is simple. Candidates must be 18 or over, unemployed or under-employed. Anyone who does not hold a high school diploma or GED certificate will be enrolled in a literacy, ABE, or GED program. Proper attendance and performance in this supplementary program is mandatory for participation in Hammerwest. Students in this drug-free program are subject to random drug testing. Hammerwest aims at providing job training for first-time and non-violent offenders referred by the courts to complete community service hours. Court referrals are combined with other neighborhood residents who are paid a stipend while engaged in training.

Partners: Westside Cooperative Organization (WESCO); Indianapolis Police Department (IPD) West District; Christamore House; Hawthorne Community Center; Westside Community Development Corp. (WCDC); Local Businesses

Youth Entrepreneurship Program

This program is designed to service youth ages 15–25. Youth are taught business-related skills such as writing a business proposal, starting up and maintaining their own business, reading spreadsheets, and understanding the stock market, as well as eight other skills covered in *Kids' Way Incorporation: A Youth Businessman's Guide and Workbook*. Participants prepare business plans to submit to Eli Lilly for possible funding for their business idea. Goal: to successfully train and graduate twenty youth each year.

Partners: Christamore House; Westside Community Ministries, Inc. (WCMI)

Recreational Programs

Haughville Roundball

Gives our neighborhood youth an opportunity to interact with the police and firefighters who service our area.

Partners: Police Athletic League (PAL) Club; Indianapolis Police Department (IPD) West District; Indianapolis Fire Department (IFD); Kroger; IndyParks

High on Life

This program provides youth ages 13–18 the opportunity to enhance self-expression, to promote life skills, and to develop and maintain a healthy life style through physical and mental exercise. The youth meet every Thursday night from 7–10 P.M. for basketball, volleyball, table tennis, chess, card games, music, and open-mike rap sessions.

Partners: Indiana Sport Corporation; Indianapolis Police Department (IPD) West District; WESCO Dads; Indianapolis Public Housing; Christamore House

Hip Hop Haven on the Road

This is a free event that offers non-violent rap, hip-hop music, and positive adult mentoring for youth. Provides a safe haven for youth on Friday and Saturday nights.

Partners: City Hill Church; Indianapolis Police Department (IPD) West District

Home Base Club

Teen volunteers provide positive team role models to youth ages 8–12. The project provides an instructional softball program and teaches participants the rules and regulations of softball.

Partners: Youth As Resources

Mind Blowing Chess

Meets one Saturday each month to train inner city youth ages 5–18 in chess tournament play. Participants become competent chess players through a series of championships, with emphasis on the most improved in each division. Chess teaches conflict resolution by first playing by the rules to involve appropriate authorities when necessary, to not be intimidated by adversaries, and to apply mental superiority instead of fists to resolve disputes.

Partners: Chess Academy Parham; Christamore House; Youth Fair Chance; Indianapolis Public Housing

Recreation Program (Open Gym)

Provides recreational opportunities for area youth. Helps youth achieve and maintain fitness through playing cooperative games and acquiring a range of physical skills while developing a sense of teamwork and fair play.

Summer Day Camp

Provides educational and recreational opportunities for WESCO youth ages 5–12. Offers various sporting activities, a weekly art program, weekly field trips, educational programs, and a daily lunch program.

Partners: IndyParks; Christamore House; National Junior Tennis League (NJTL); Indiana Sports Corporation; Americorps

Teens General Social Development

14 youth enrolled in "Grasshoppers" (martial arts), 12 youth enrolled in boxing, 29 youth enrolled in open gym, 24 enrolled in life skills (CHAP/CHAT), and 24 enrolled in tutoring.

WESCO/Weed & Seed Recreation Program

Tutoring, open gym, field trips, teen court, community service, and special events at IPD West District.

Partners: Indianapolis Police Department (IPD) West District; Indiana University-Purdue University-Indianapolis (IUPUI) Work Study Students; Reach for Youth; Atkins Boys & Girls Club

Health & Environmental Programs

Aerobics

Beginning and advanced fitness program for youth and adults.
Partners: Healthy Start

Green Thumb Club

A community service corps of youth, serving neighborhood seniors. Activities have included yardwork and neighborhood clean-ups.
Partners: Keep Indianapolis Beautiful; Sheffield Manor

Strategic War Against Trash (SWAT)

A summer program that involves four to seven 17- and 18-year-old residents in a 10-week program in the summer. Participants are expected to attend social development classes as part of their work. The program helps supplement their education and prepares them for the job force.

Westside Extravaganza

A Health Fair, IPD Good Grades Carnival, and a Community Awareness Day. This event rewards Westside students for earning good grades and lets the community know what services are available to them.

Partners: MOM Project; Indianapolis Police Department (IPD) West District

Substance Abuse & Crime Prevention Programs

BABES

A drug and alcohol awareness program for 4- to 11-year-olds using puppets. It consists of 7 sessions.

Community Unity March Against Violence & Drugs

Residents and churches on the Near Westside are taking the initiative in speaking out against drug activity in their neighborhoods. They were willing to take a stand and started an Anti-Drug March. This event furthers the work of creating a safer environment for residents on the Near Westside of the city.

Partners: Indianapolis Public Housing Agency; Speedway Police; U.S. Marshall; Indiana University-Purdue University-Indianapolis (IUPUI) Police; Indy Park Rangers; Indiana State Police; Indianapolis Police Department; Community Residents

McGruff & Officer Friendly

A police officer and McGruff visit with children in their classroom and show a video. There are three video sessions: safety, gangs, and drugs.

Partners: Indianapolis Police Department (IPD) West District; Hawthorne Community Center; Holy Trinity; Carrie's Day Care; Christamore House; Head Start; Unique 7

No Is Not Enough (NINE)

This program is geared to youth ages 4–18 and offers age-appropriate drug prevention and communication skill workshops, a youth forum, and a youth support-group. It is staffed with concerned parents, certified substance abuse counselors, social workers, and other volunteers who believe to "just say no" is not enough unless youth have something to say YES to!

Resurrection of Hope Center

Center for young adults and youth counseling. Provides intervention services to reduce youth substance abuse and drug dealing.

Teen Court

A peer sentencing program for juvenile offenders. Youth ages 10–17 participate as prosecuting attorneys, defense counsels, bailiff, court clerk, and jury; 85 percent of offenders complete their sentences and commit no future crimes.

Partners: Youth As Resources

assumes a familiarity w/
Indianapolis.

"Time sequence"
    out of order
Kids ages don't
match examples, personal,
for instance (p. 110) Olgen's
school years.